The Origin and Nature of our Institutional Models

Wolf Wolfensberger

Human Policy Press

Designed by Leslie Prince

The Center on Human Policy also gratefully acknowledges the permission of the Syracuse Developmental Center for entree and use of its historical archives.

© 1975   Human Policy Press
P.O. Box 127
University Station
Syracuse, New York 13210

Send for complete list of publications from Human Policy Press. Bulk rates available on all publications.

FOREWORD

In 1968, Wolf Wolfensberger wrote "The Origin and Nature of Our Institutional Models" for a larger publication entitled *Changing Patterns in Residential Services for the Mentally Retarded,* published by the President's Committee on Mental Retardation. That publication attempted an historic task, to document and chart a movement of change toward the normalization of services for the so-called retarded.

Just as Wolfensberger found the sage warnings of Howe and Dix about the dangers of institutionalization to be startlingly contemporary, so too can we look to Wolfensberger's own history of institutions as a remarkably timely perspective from which to view our present efforts at transforming institutions. Wolfensberger wrote his chronicle in 1968, yet the issues he raised are as important today as ever. Despite countless documentaries of institutional life, exposed by a conscientious media, and recent lawsuits on the right to treatment in institutions, the society continues to spawn institutional structures.

The text bears much relevance not only because of its critique of the institutional model but also for its insightful explanation of the ideologies and assumptions which have led to and justified institutions. In this sense, Wolfensberger's history is as useful to the community service person as to the institutional attendant. Perhaps more so, in fact, for as human service workers become advocates for the "retarded," as we develop plans to integrate people with special needs into the larger society, as we formulate vocational, recreational, and residential programs in the community, it is essential that we understand the effects of our ideologies on those whom we intend to serve. Lest future observers look back on present day programs and treatment models as instruments of cruelty and, more importantly, lest people suffer unduly as a result of our ignorance, we must adopt a self-critical pose; we must examine our attitudes and plans in the manner that Wolfensberger suggests.

Through a better understanding of how institutions emerged and through a complementary understanding of what normalization entails, we can work toward and perhaps truly witness what Wolfensberger called the "agonizing death struggle of the institutional model."

Douglas Biklen

Syracuse, New York 1973

AUTHOR'S PREFACE
TO THE REVISED VERSION OF THIS MONOGRAPH

The pressure of other demands have prevented me from re-editing and updating this monograph, except for correcting some errors and typing mistakes, and for some minor stylistic and vocabulary improvements. A number of the names of various historical figures are still spelled wrongly in this chapter. The problem is that some of their names were spelled incorrectly in their own publications (as seems to have been the case with Nosworthy (1907) which should probably be Norsworthy; or they were spelled inconsistently, as with Murdoch (1903, 1906, 1909) versus Murdock (1917, 1913). In consequence, I have generally used the spelling that is consistent with the reference (source) used, which has the advantage of aiding in bibliographic retrieval.

Since this monograph was originally written as a chapter for *Changing Patterns in Residential Services for the Mentally Retarded* (1969), a major new historic text has appeared (Ludmerer, K. M. *Genetics and American Society.* Baltimore: Johns Hopkins University Press, (1972). Anyone with an interest in the development of the "genetic alarm" movement is urged to read it; it provides further evidence of the trends posited in this monograph.

The monograph is also being republished as a chapter by the President's Committee on Mental Retardation in a revised edition of *Changing Patterns in Residential Services for the Mentally Retarded.* The reader is further advised that Part 1 of the chapter, plus the contents of all or part of several of the chapters (by Nirje and Dybwad) in the 1969 edition of *Changing Patterns* have been generalized beyond mental retardation to deviancy in general, expanded, and incorporated in a text on *The Principle of Normalization in Human Services* (Wolfensberger, W. Toronto: National Institute on Mental Retardation, 1972). A further revision and expansion of that text is foreseen.

Acknowledgement

The Center on Human Policy gratefully acknowledges the permission of the President's Committee on Mental Retardation to reprint this adapted historical account from *Changing Patterns in Residential Services for the Mentally Retarded* (Washington: PCMR, 1969), edited by Robert B. Kugel and Wolf Wolfensberger.

A NOTE ABOUT THE PHOTOGRAPHS...

Responding to a photograph is a very individual experience. As "viewers" we each bring our own experiences, values, and attitudes to the visual page. We can choose to respond to some, all, or none of what we see. We filter out the intellectual, emotional and aesthetic qualities as we see fit. With an historical photograph, we filter our reactions through the special perspective of time. If we do not like what we see, we can turn away and say, "It did not *really* happen, or if it did, well, it was so long ago!" We can use the passage of time to diffuse the ugliness or even hide the unpleasantness and deny that it ever existed.

The same is true of the issues presented in Wolfensberger's text. It is a personal experience, with each reader responding to some, all, or none of what they read. At first I found the story so incredulous that my reaction was disbelief. How could humanitarian intentions produce such a dehumanizing monster? I could no longer hide my disbelief when I discovered the hundreds of pictures from which these photographs were selected. Seeing the people and places with my own eyes forced me to realize that this history is a true chronicle of humanity: a real story with real people and places.

These pictures were commissioned by the institutions. Professional photographers actually posed the people and situations. We can, therefore, assume that the majority of these shots were used to promote the best aspects of institutional care. As the public relations photos of the day, they reflect the precise imagery that administrators wished to accentuate and preserve.

As this book goes to print, two hundred thousand people reside in institutions for the "retarded" across America. The nightmare of the institution (known as "asylum," "state school," or "developmental center") has not faded into a closed chapter of history. Are we any different from our predecessors? Has our modern architectural technology camouflaged the truth of our own times? Will we have to wait 100 years for others to perceive our actions in the same way that we view those of earlier reformers?

This historical documentation is only a means to an end. Perhaps it will serve as a catalyst for us to examine ourselves and our personal convictions.

> Our chief concern with the past is not what we have done, nor the adventures we have met but the moral reaction of bygone events within ourselves.
>
> Jane Addams, *The Long Road of Woman's Memory*, 1917, p. 101.

Madeline Bragar
Syracuse, 1975

Table of Contents

	Page
CHAPTER 1 THE LANGUAGE OF ARCHITECTURE	1
The Perception of the Retarded Person's Role as a Determinant of the Institutional Models	2
The Retarded Person as Sick	5
The Retarded Person as a Subhuman Organism	7
The Retarded Person as a Menace	13
The Retarded Person as an Object of Pity	13
The Retarded Person as a Burden of Charity	14
The Retarded Person as a Holy Innocent	14
The Retarded Person as a Developing Individual	15
Other Roles of Retarded Persons	17
The Meaning of a Building	17
The Building as a Monument	19
The Building as a Public Relations Medium	19
The Building as a Medium of Service	20
The Focus of Convenience of a Building	20
The Convenience of the Architect	20
The Convenience of the Community	20
The Convenience of the Staff	21
The Convenience of the Resident	21
CHAPTER 2 THE EVOLUTION OF INSTITUTIONAL MODELS IN THE UNITED STATES	23
Making Deviant Individuals Undeviant	24
Protecting Deviant Individuals from Nondeviant People	27

	Page
Protecting Nondeviant Individuals from Deviant People	33
The Early Indictment	33
The Peak of the Indictment	34
Dehumanizing and Brutalizing Elements of the Indictment	36
Concern with Prevention	38
Failure of Preventive Marriage Laws	39
Failure of Preventive Sterilization	40
Failure of Preventive Segregation	41
Failure to Support Community Alternatives to Segregation	53
The End of the Indictment	54
Momentum Without Rationales	55
CHAPTER 3 THE REALITIES OF INSTITUTIONAL ACCOMPLISHMENTS	59
APPENDIX 1	70
APPENDIX 2	80
REFERENCES	84
FOOTNOTES	88

Chapter 1
The Language of Architecture

In 1854, this institution for "feebleminded" persons was one of the first to be built in North America. In 1916 Kirkbride called for us to remember "that our purpose is not to build costly monuments at the expense of the taxpayer, to architects, legislators, and governors or indeed to ourselves." In 1970, on this exact site, the 1854's replacement was constructed at a cost of 23 million dollars.

There is probably little disagreement that aside from considerations of cost, or of the nature of the prospective residents, the design of residential facilities for the retarded is affected by attitudes and philosophies held by the designers and those who guide and direct them. These attitudes and philosophies may be held without the holder being conscious of their presence. Indeed, the holder may verbally and vehemently deny holding an attitude or philosophy which is strongly expressed in a building.

There are at least three dimensions of attitudes and philosophies that can be discerned in building design. These are: (1) the role expectancies the building design and atmosphere impose upon prospective residents, (2) the meaning embodied in or conveyed by a building, and (3) the focus of convenience designed into the building, i.e., whether the building was designed primarily with the convenience of the residents, the community, the staff, or the architect in mind.

Each of these three dimensions will be discussed below. However, the reader is reminded that the three dimensions are arbitrary ways of conceptualizing or analyzing the situation, and features which may be characteristic of one part of one dimension may be found to characterize parts of other dimensions. Additional dimensions can be defined with equal validity, although those defined here were felt to have particularly salient relevance to the present topic.

The term "model" will be encountered frequently in this essay. A human management model is here defined as a consistent pattern in which the behavior of persons is structured by other persons who exercise authority over them. A residential or institutional model consists of the interaction of the physical environment of the residence with the behavioral roles that managers impose upon or elicit from the managed residents.

THE PERCEPTION OF THE RETARDED PERSON'S ROLE AS A DETERMINANT OF THE INSTITUTIONAL MODELS

A person's social perceptions are profoundly influenced by his basic values and orientation to life. Certain of these values and orientations have clear-cut implications to one's perception or image of the retarded person and his role. And one's image of the retarded person has definite implications to one's conceptualization of the residential service model appropriate for persons cast into the retarded role.

As Shakespeare said:

"All the world's a stage,
And all the men and women merely players;
They have their exits and their entrances;
And one man in his time plays many parts."
(*As You Like It.* Act II, Scene VII, 139-142)

It is a well-established fact that a person's behavior tends to be profoundly affected by the role expectations that are placed upon him. Generally, people will play the roles that they have been assigned. This permits those who define social roles to make self-fulfilling prophecies by predicting that someone cast into a certain role will emit behavior consistent with that role. Unfortunately, role-appropriate behavior will then often be interpreted to be a person's "natural" rather than elicited mode of acting.

In institutions, role performance is influenced not only by the interpersonal stimuli to which an institution resident might be exposed on the part of the institution personnel, but also by the opportunities and demands of the physical environment. For instance, the environment can very clearly express the expectation that a resident is not supposed to assume any responsibility for his actions, or that he is expected to act out violently, etc. By the same token, the physical environment may impose a demand for controlled and highly socialized behavior which is clearly communicated to the prospective resident.

Social scientists in the recent past have elaborated a concept of great importance to the understanding of the behavior and management of retarded persons. The concept is that of "deviance." A person can be defined as being deviant if he is perceived as being significantly different from others in some overt aspect, and if this difference is negatively valued. An overt and negatively valued characteristic is called a "stigma."

The handicapped person is usually seen as deviant, and expected to play a deviant role. The retarded person, being handicapped and often multiply stigmatized, is deviant by definition. Too often, our texts have tried to explain attitudes toward the retarded in a narrow sense. However, to understand trends within our field, and society's response to the retarded, one must first understand societal attitudes toward deviancy generally, because a wide range of deviances may elicit similar responses or expectancy patterns from people.

Wilkins (1965) suggests that our attitudes toward deviance derive from the Platonic notion that goodness, truth, and beauty are related to each other, and that deviations from norms (truth) are "errors" that, by analogy, must be related to evil and ugliness. Thus, attitudes toward deviance may be rather generalized. For instance, a person may react with similar emotions toward retardation as he does toward blindness, delinquency, and old age.

It is chastening to recall that the retarded in American history were long grouped with other types of deviant groups. In early America, the Puritans looked with suspicion on any deviation from behavioral norms, and irregular conduct was often explained in terms of the supernatural, such as witchcraft. There is reason to believe that retarded individuals were hanged and burned on this suspicion. Later in New England, records show that lunatics, "distracted" persons, people who were *non compos mentis*, and those who had "fits" were all classed together, perhaps, with vagabonds and paupers thrown in (Deutsch, 1949). Connecticut's first house of correction in 1722 was for rogues, vagabonds, the idle, beggars, fortune tellers, diviners, musicians, runaways, drunkards, prostitutes, pilferers, brawlers—and the mentally afflicted (Deutsch, 1949). As late as about 1820, the retarded, together with other dependent deviant groups such as aged paupers, the sick poor, or the mentally distracted were publicly "sold" ("bid off") to the *lowest* bidder, i.e., bound over to the person who offered to take responsibility for them for the lowest amount of public support (Deutsch, 1949).

The 10th (1880) U.S. census first combined "defectives," "dependents," and "delinquents" for reporting purposes. The Public Health Service combined "criminals, defectives, and delinquents" as late as the 1920's.

The National Conference on Charities and Correction, between about 1875 and 1920, often grouped the idiotic, imbecilic and feeble-minded with the deaf, dumb, blind, epileptic, insane, delinquent and offenders into one general class of "defectives." Few of us today are aware of the fact that the more contemporary term "mental defective" was coined to distinguish the retarded from these other "defectives," and it is no coincidence that many state institutions were for both the retarded and the epileptic. During the "indictment period," discussed later, an incredible range of deviances were associated with retardation; indeed, they were seen to be caused by it: illness; physical impediments; poverty; vagrancy; unemployment; alcoholism; sex offenses of various types, including prostitution and illegitimacy; crime; mental illness; and epilepsy. All these were called the "degeneracies."

"The chronic insane, the epileptic, the paralytic, the imbecile and idiot of various grades, the moral imbecile, the sexual pervert, the kleptomaniac; many, if not most, of the chronic inebriates; many of the prostitutes, tramps and minor criminals; many habitual paupers, especially the ignorant and irresponsible mothers of illegitimate children, so common in poor houses; many of the shiftless poor, ever on the verge of pauperism and often stepping over into it; some of the blind, some deaf-mutes, some consumptives. All these classes, in varying degree with others not mentioned, are related as being effects of the one cause—which itself is the summing up of many causes—'degeneracy'" (quoted by Johnson, 1903, p. 246).

The first institutions for the retarded were built in a period of optimism regarding mental illness and the education of the deaf and blind, and many facilities for these other deviant groups were erected at that time. The later disillusionment about retardation was also not isolated, but part of a more generalized aversion toward, and virtual persecution of, deviances. Farm colonies were a logical development in mental retardation, but were also part of the history of mental institutions of the same period. During the early part of the century—a very chauvinistic period—numerous writers claimed that a large proportion of retarded persons came from foreign-born stock, contributing to the call for more restrictive immigration laws. This is perhaps an extreme example of how retardation was linked in the minds of many to other types of deviance. One could go on endlessly demonstrating the point that societal responses toward retardation were not specific, but were part of a more generalized pattern of response toward deviancy.

Historically, deviancy has been handled in a number of ways.

1. Deviancy can be prevented. A psycho-social means of prevention is not to attach negative value to certain types of differentness. For instance, medieval Catholicism and the more contemporary Hutterites (a religious sect related to the Amish, living a communal life, mostly in the prairie area) did not place excessive value on intellectual achievement, and therefore were less likely to view the retarded as deviant.

2. Deviancy can be made undeviant, usually by means such as education, training, and treatment.

3. Deviant groups, being perceived as unpleasant, offensive or frightening can be segregated from the mainstream of society and placed at its periphery. We have numerous examples of this in our society: we segregate Indians in reservations, and Negroes in the ghetto; the aged are congregated in special homes, ostensibly for their own good, and these homes are often located at the periphery of our communities or in the country; deaf and blind children who could be taught in the regular schools are sent to residential schools, many of which are on the periphery of, or remote from population centers; we have (or have had) "dying rooms" in our hospitals to save us the unpleasantness of ultimate deviancy; and the emotionally disturbed and the retarded may be placed in institutions far in the countryside.

Deviancy can be seen to be someone's fault or perhaps a sign that the deviant person's parents had sinned and were being punished by the Lord. The belief that blemish in the offspring is the result of punishment for parental wrongdoing appears to be deeply ingrained in the unconscious of the people. Often, this belief is overtly expressed. It is a belief that had been held by Howe (a leading American pioneer in the field of retardation) and was repeatedly expressed by him. In fact, he even asserted that retardation could result from a person's own wrongdoing (Howe, 1848, 1852, 1866), e.g.: "It appeared to us certain that the existence of so many idiots in every generation must be the consequence of some violation of the *natural laws;*—that where there was so much suffering, there must have been sin" (1848, p. 4). Greene (1884, p. 270) said: "Our wards are innocent of crime or fault. In the large majority of instances, they are the feeble and deformed expressions of parental sins or sorrows." Parental alcoholism, for instance, was widely believed to be a major cause of retardation (e.g., Kerlin, 1886, p. 297). Perceived to be the result of sin, deviance is something to be ashamed of, hidden, and "put away." The puritans held views along these lines (Deutsch, 1949).

4. Deviancy can be destroyed. In the past, some kinds of deviancy were seen to be the work of the devil or other evil forces. As such, the deviant person was evil too, and had to be persecuted and destroyed so as to protect society. Destruction of deviant individuals may also be advocated for other reasons such as self-preservation or self-protection. For instance, many societies have condoned the destruction of weaker, less adequate, or handicapped members. This was true of ancient Greece and Rome, of the Eskimos and bushmen, and of Nazi Germany. In the United States, the increasing sentiment for, and legalization of, abortion of high-risk fetuses can be viewed, at least in part, as a variant of this theme.

In one's professional functioning, in the literature, and in the history of the field, one can discern at least seven well-defined role perceptions of the mentally retarded. Most of these roles are deviant ones. The relationship between these role perceptions, and management of the retarded, and the design of their life space, though of crucial significance, is not always obvious. I will attempt to demonstrate how location, architecture, interior appointments, and day-to-day operating procedures of institutions will tend to form interrelated patterns (management models) that are consistent with various role perceptions of retardation.[2] Institutional models based on seven major role perceptions of the retarded will be discussed.

The Retarded Person as Sick

One of the most prominent role perceptions of the retarded individual has been that of the sick person. The literature is replete with statements such as Fernald's (1915, p. 96): "The biological, economic and sociological bearings of feeble-mindedness have overshadowed the fact that it is fundamentally and essentially a medical question." An unequivocal more contemporary restatement of this role perception is contained in a very important document, viz., the *Mental Retardation Handbook for the Primary Physician*, issued by the American Medical Association (1965). In this work, mental retardation is repeatedly identified as a "disease" (e.g., p. 98) or an "illness" (e.g., p. 47).

When the retarded are viewed as diseased organisms, residential facilities are structured on the (medical) hospital model. This model tends to have the following characteristics:

1. The facility is administered by a medical hierarchy: the chief administrative officer (e.g., the superintendent) is a physician, with a hierarchy of other physicians under him, and a hierarchy of nurses under them. Concern about authority lines tends to result in a tightly controlled perpendicular administrative structure rather than a flexible subunitized one.

2. The residence is identified or even labeled, at least in part, as a hospital (e.g., "state hospital and school").

3. Living units are referred to as nursing units or wards.

4. Residents are referred to as patients, and their retardation is identified as being a "disease" that requires a "diagnosis" and "prognosis."

5. Resident care is referred to as nursing care.

6. Case records are referred to as charts.

7. Hospital routines prevail. For example, admission procedures may require days or weeks of "observation" and residence in an "infirmary" or similar unit prior to "diagnosis" and to assignment to regular living quarters. Daily routines may resemble hospital routines in regard to rising, body inspections, sick call, charting, etc.; indeed, the daily schedule may revolve around the hinge of medication schedules. Dispensing of medication, in turn, may become the model for intake of nourishment, and for other "treatments" as well. Such other treatments, even if "administered" in the form of education, may be referred to as "dosages." Usually, there is at least moderate emphasis upon convenience of "nursing care."

8. Concern with professional status symbols and status differentiation often encountered in a hospital atmosphere may be expressed by features such as presence of hierarchical staff lounges, showers, and private toilets. There may be separate vending machines for staff and "patients." Staff and residents rarely eat together. Caretaker personnel may wear uniforms. Even professional and semiprofessional personnel may wear uniforms, coats of different colors, badges, name plates with their degrees listed, and similar insignia of their role and rank.

9. Nonmedical personnel may emulate the medical role, e.g., social workers and psychologists may wear white coats or jackets, and prestigious professionals may be referred to as "doctor" even if they do not possess a doctorate degree.

10. Resident management programs are re-

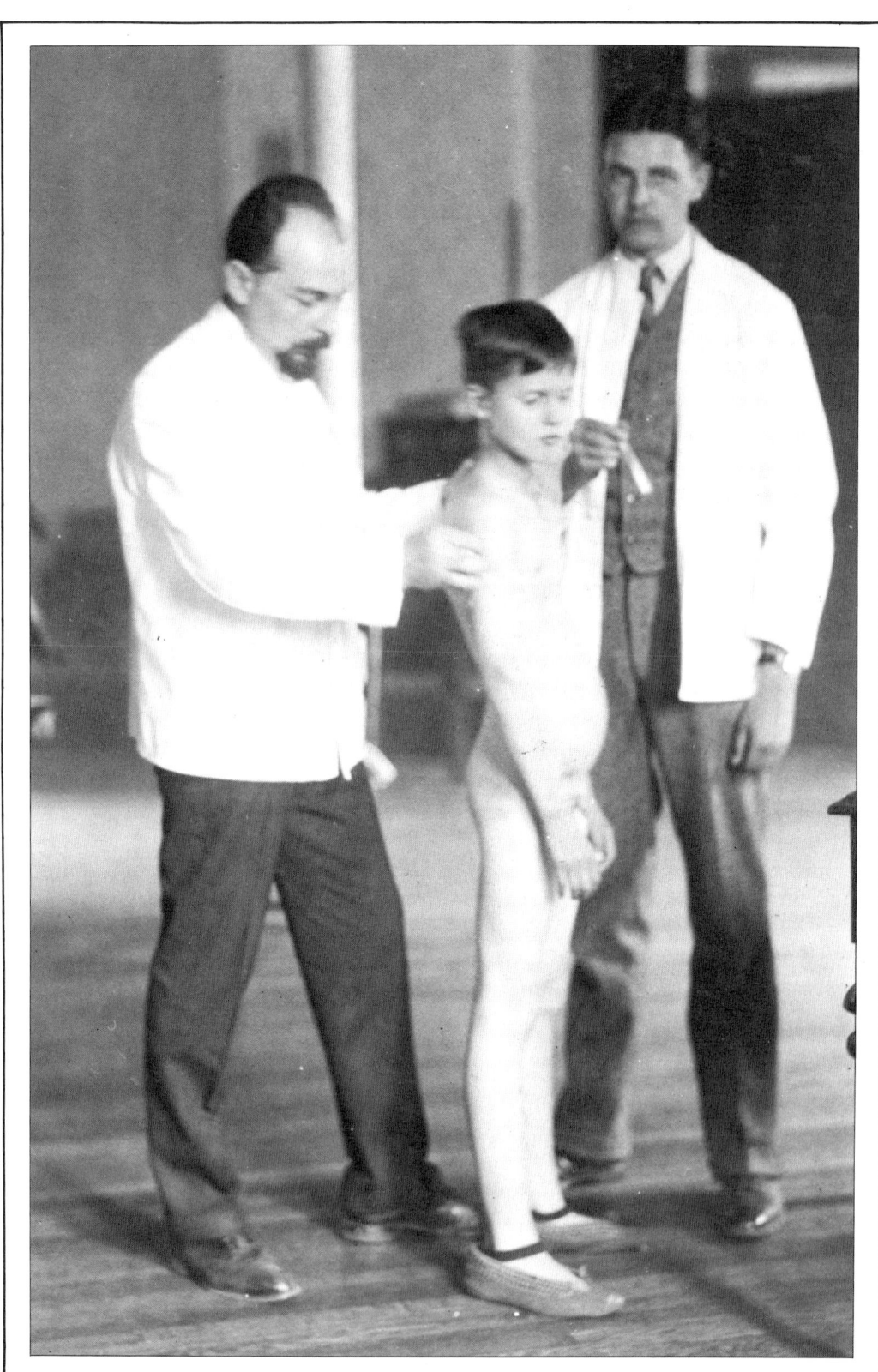

ferred to as "treatments" or "therapy," e.g., recreation and work assignments may become recreational and industrial therapy. Even ordinary schooling may become educational therapy.

11. Physicians, whether qualified or not, make decisions about nonmedical matters, e.g., residents' rights and privileges; visits; work assignments; discipline; inclusion in school, training, and other programs. Even if these decisions are made by nonmedical personnel (perhaps because of temporary or permanent lack of physician manpower), this may be perceived as delegation of medical authority, and as such is perceived and interpreted as undesirable and transient.

12. Departments with the greatest affinity to medicine are given priority in program development, e.g., dentistry, orthopedics, and physical therapy may receive stronger support than behavior shaping, education, etc.

13. Physical and medical techniques are more likely to be used in managing the behavior of residents than other techniques. Thus, disturbed residents are more likely to be physically restricted or settled with drugs than to be counseled or trained; residents with seizures may be placed on anticonvulsant medication with little thought given to environmental manipulation of seizure-precipitating events or to educating the person to develop preventive behavior habits.

14. There exists an excessive abhorrence of any chance or likelihood of injury to the resident. On the one hand, this is exemplified by lack of stairs and steps, sharp objects and corners, conventional electrical outlets, access to conventional hot water faucets, etc. On the other hand, it is exemplified by the presence of special features such as ramps, screening of radiators, and screened stairways (if any).

15. A disease conceptualization of retardation

Because retardation was defined as "fundamentally and essentially a medical question," a resident, upon admission to the institution, was examined by the chief administrative officers, the physicians. Here a child's measurements are recorded. (1925)

tends to result in a management dilemma. On the one hand, such a conceptualization often results in pursuit of treatment hoped to result in cure; on the other hand, unless a "cure" is seen as likely, the management atmosphere is often permeated with hopelessness and treatment nihilism. In other words, the disease conceptualization tends to be correlated with inappropriate extremes of management attitudes.

The Retarded Person as a Subhuman Organism

The fact that deviant subgroups within a culture may be perceived as not fully human has long been recognized. To this day, large segments of our population deny full humanity to members of certain minority groups such as Negroes [blacks] and American Indians. The retarded are particularly apt to be unconsciously perceived or even consciously labeled as subhuman, as animal-like, or even as "vegetables" or "vegetative."

The literature of the field is richly endowed with labels alluding to the alleged subhuman nature of the retarded. The term "garden variety," widely used by professionals in the field to refer to cultural-familial retardation, has definite vegetative connotations. It is interesting to note that the vegetable concept may, in part, have been derived from an inappropriate transfer of the medical concept of "vegetative functions." In medicine, the "vital functions" controlled by the autonomic nervous system and/or the hypothalamus may be referred to as "vegetative." These functions, which include temperature, heart rate, blood pressure, respiration rate, etc., are possessed by all humans and most animal species, and yet the concept of vegetative functions appears to have been translated into the social context in such a way as to abrogate even the animal, not to mention human, qualities of a person.

Luther, in describing what appears to have been a severely or profoundly retarded child, denied the child's humanity as follows: "Eight years ago, there was one at Dessau whom I, Martinus Luther, saw and grappled with. He was twelve years old, had the use of his eyes and all his senses, so that one might think that he was a normal child. But he did nothing but gorge himself as much as four peasants or threshers. He ate, defecated and drooled and, if anyone tackled him, he screamed. If things didn't go well, he wept. So I said to the Prince of Anhalt: 'If I were the Prince, I should take this child to the Molda River which flows near Dessau and drown him.' But the Prince of Anhalt and the Prince of Saxony, who happened to be present, refused to follow my advice. Thereupon I said: 'Well, then the Christians shall order the Lord's Prayer to be said in church and pray that the dear Lord take the Devil away.' This was done daily in Dessau and the changeling died in the following year. When Luther was asked why he had made such a recommendation, he replied that he was firmly of the opinion that such changelings were merely a mass of flesh, a *massa carnis,* with no soul. 'For it is the Devil's power that he corrupts people who have reason and souls when he possesses them. The Devil sits in such changelings where their soul should have been!'"[3]

Deutsch (1949) pointed out that by some peculiar twist of logic, the mentally ill were often apt to be stripped of their human attributes, together with their rights and privileges as human beings. Obviously, it is even easier to dehumanize a person who never possessed much reason if one dehumanizes him who had reason but lost it. The idea that the mentally afflicted lack sensory acuity, e.g., that they are insensitive to heat and cold, was popular into the mid-1800's (Deutsch, 1949). This myth resulted in their often being denied heat during the winter in the cold cells of institutions, and may well have contributed to the image of the retarded as insensate vegetables. To this day, retarded persons, like army recruits, may be said to need "being broken" or tamed, like horses or wild beasts. Just recently (*Atlantic Monthly,* October 1967, p. 49) a reader called for the " . . . sacrifice of mentally defective humans, or human vegetables . . . " to provide organ transplants and " . . . increase the intellectual betterment of mankind . . . " Dehumanization of the retarded is so accepted, even to this day, and even by workers in our own field, that we witness a public statement by a contemporary superintendent of a state institution referring to his retarded charges as " . . . so-called human beings. . . " " . . . below what we might call an animal level of functioning . . . " (*Frontiers of Hospital Psychiatry,* 1968, 5, 5-6).

The atmosphere and design of a residential facility can very clearly express an expectancy that the resident will behave in a subhuman fashion—no matter how vociferously the staff may deny adherence to dehumanizing attitudes. Such expectancies are implicit in any of virtually hundreds of dehumanizing practices encountered in institutions and enumerated by Vail (1967). Some of the more common expectancies will be listed and briefly elucidated here.

1. The perception of the retarded as animals usually implies an expectation that they behave in a primitive, uncontrolled fashion. Thus, the environment is designed to be "abuse-resistant," which implies measures such as:
   (a) Walls, floors, etc., made of material that is indestructible.
   (b) Unbreakable, shatterproof or wire-enmeshed glass in windows and partitions.
   (c) Installation of the sturdiest, most heavy-duty furniture and equipment.
   (d) Minimization of moving parts.
   (e) High ceilings with recessed or specially shielded or laminated light fixtures, to minimize damage due to throwing of objects.
   (f) Soundproofing to muffle the sounds residents are expected to emit; such soundproofing may even be installed in areas designed for persons quite capable of learning adaptive behavior.
   (g) Television sets protected by wire screens, recessed into protective housing, and/or placed above reach.

2. A presumably subhuman individual is usually perceived as being potentially assaultive, de-

structive, and lacking in self-direction and constructive purpose; this necessitates restricting his movements both to control him more easily and to protect either the human from the subhuman, or one subhuman from another. This characteristically leads to a number of measures.

(a) Locked living units.
(b) Locked areas within living units. In the case of children or the physically handicapped, door knobs may be set high and above reach, or complicated release mechanisms may be installed. This permits staff to perceive the facility as "open" even though it is *de facto* locked.
(c) Doors made from heavy material; bedroom doors can be locked only from the outside, and often open outward rather than inward as in most homes or offices.
(d) Barred windows. More sophisticated but equally effective are the reinforced window screens, or so-called security screening.
(e) Outdoor play areas enclosed by either high walls or high, strong fences or by both. Often, these areas are quite small (and therefore, easier to control), and not sufficiently large, or equipped, for adequate exercise. Such small areas again permit the staff to engage in conscience-salving self-deception. I once inquired of a nurse whether the children in her locked living unit were ever dressed up and taken outdoors. She assured me that the children were dressed and taken for outdoor walks every day. The woman was not hypocritical; she was only rephrasing reality so that she could live with it. The reality was that these moderately to severely retarded ambulatory children did not leave the building confines for months, perhaps years, at a time. "Dressing" meant to put on more clothes than underpants and diapers; and "going for a walk outdoors" meant being turned loose in large groups with minimal supervision in a small outdoor enclave enclosed by high brick walls on two sides and high wire fences on the other two sides.
(f) A fence or wall surrounding entire buildings or even an entire facility complex.
(g) Segregation of sexes. Such segregation may assume absurd proportions when practices with infants and children, or with the aged retarded.

A typical programmatic, rather than architectural, expression of the subhuman view surrounds the "feeding" of residents. To this day, food and drink may be served in unbreakable tin reminiscent of prison riot films of the 1930's. Often no knives and forks are permitted. The latter measure also necessitates the serving of special foods, such as finger foods or soft homogenized pap that can be spooned.

3. Since the perceived subhuman is not believed to be capable of meaningful controlled choice behavior, he is permitted minimal control over his environment. This typically implies the following:

(a) Switches controlling the lights of resident areas such as dayrooms, sleeping quarters, toilets, etc., are made inaccessible to residents by placement in staff control areas such as nursing stations, placement in locked cabinets, or keying (i.e., a key is required to turn a light on or off).
(b) Water temperature in lavatories, showers, etc., is controlled by thermostats. The water flow itself may be controlled by staff by means of removable and portable handles.
(c) Temperature, humidity, and air movement controls are locked or keyed.
(d) Radiators are locked, recessed, or screened.
(e) Residents are usually forbidden to carry matches or lighters.

4. Perception of the retarded as animals implies

an emphasis on efficient "keeping" of residents, rather than on interaction with personnel. Consequently, the environment is designed for efficient supervision.

(a) Staff work behind isolating (protective?) partitions which keep out residents and perhaps even their sounds, but permit extensive or complete visual monitoring. A stated rationale here may be that isolation makes for greater efficiency in certain caretaker tasks such as visual supervision, record keeping, and administration of medications.

(b) Residents sleep in large dormitories, with no or only low partitions between beds. Lights may burn even at night to facilitate supervision.

(c) Staff emphasize tasks which minimize chances for interaction. For example, supervisory staff may be isolated in a separate building. Living units may be widely dispersed and removed so that ready interaction between staff and residents is difficult to achieve; in one such widely dispersed residential complex I have known, low staff interaction with residents was partially due to the fact that walking was both time-consuming and often not feasible due to bad weather, and driving was inconvenient because of lack of parking space near the residential units. Even staff meetings and in-service training activities can become an unconscious legitimization of noninteraction with residents.

(d) There is much emphasis on use of drugs (chemical straightjackets?), rather than human interaction, to control and shape behavior.

(e) The placement of residential centers far from population centers and towns can, in some cases, be a correlate of a "keeping" or "controlling" desire.

5. Subhumans are perceived to "live like animals," i.e., to soil themselves and their habitat. This results in the design of an environment that can be cleaned easily, frequently, efficiently, and on a massive scale:

(a) Walls and floors may be made of a material that is virtually impossible to "deface," i.e., scratch, soil, stain, etc., and that can be hosed down (like in a zoo); there may be drains in the floors of living areas.

(b) Beds and bed stalls may be designed to be picked up and immersed in cleansing solutions in their entirety by means of cranes.

(c) Resident bathing facilities may be designed for efficient cleansing of large numbers of residents by small numbers of caretakers; there may be slabs, hoses, and mass showers, rather than installations conducive to self-conconducted cleansing, or the learning thereof.

6. Typically, subhuman residents are either not expected to learn or develop appreciably, or their growth potential is seen as so small as to be irrelevant, since it will never lead to complete "humanization." In other words, the state of subhumanity is perceived as being essentially permanent. In consequence, the environment is designed to maintain a resident's level of functioning, but not to provide opportunities for further growth and development.

7. Animals have no rights; it follows that residents perceived to lack humanity are also perceived to lack certain rights. Among these are:

(a) The right to privacy. Toilets and showers for the retarded may lack partitions, curtains, or doors. Bedrooms often lack doors, not to mention that the bedrooms themselves may be lacking. Where doors exist, they almost always have window panes or so-called "Judas-windows" (complete with wire-enmeshed glass or peepholes). Private visiting space may be nonexisting.

(b) The right to property. Institutionalized persons may have few or no possessions. Often they have no space to store

"Of late we have recognized a higher type of defective, the moron, and have discovered that he is a burden; that he is responsible to a large degree for many if not all of our social problems."
(about 1920)

possessions, or lack ready access to such space or control over it. Residents are usually denied the privilege of locking up their possessions, carrying the key, and using it without restrictions. Children typically do not have use of personalized clothing, and children of the same size (sometimes of various sizes) may share the same pool of clothes. All of these points have implications as to architectural design, especially regarding space allocations and selection of built-in furniture. Residents may be seen as not entitled to pay for their work, or to carry actual currency even if they do own money. "Poverty in a mental hospital is no less dehumanizing than in a slum..." (Bartlett, 1967, p. 92).

(c) The right to communicate freely. There may be censorship of incoming and outgoing mail, although some forms of censorship may not be perceived as constituting censorship. Telephone usage may be severely restricted. Visiting is usually restricted for several weeks after admission.

(d) The right to individuality. As described so well by Vail (1967), residents are regimented and managed in groups, even where individual management might be feasible. For example, residents are mass-showered where education for individual showering is possible; residents may even be mass-toileted, which accounts for the fact that some living units have more toilet seats than would be needed for, say, an equivalent-sized college dormitory.

8. The assumption that the retarded lack esthetic sense is a subtle but important corollary of the subhuman view. This corrolary results in the creation of unattractive residential living environment, since funds spent on beauty are seen as wasted. The drab, monotonous design and furnishing of residences of the retarded (sometimes in contrast to staff living quarters) is usually a testimony to this view. Rarely does one see furniture that is both comfortable and attractive in lines and color in institutions for the retarded, and even yet more rarely is there furniture-zoning so that the furniture reflects the mood and function of different living areas in an attractive fashion.

The degree to which retarded persons can appreciate beauty is really only one of two important issues involved here. The second important issue is that observers' (e.g., the public's or employees') attitudes are shaped by the context in which the retarded are presented to them. Even if intellectual limitation does impair the esthetic sense of retarded persons to deprive their environment of beauty is likely to predispose an observer to view them as subhuman.

Staff sometimes claim that drabness is due to lack of funds, but this is often untrue because much beauty can be provided at little or no cost. In my own institutional work, I recall trying to mount attractive pictures on walls of several children's living units that had a severely deprived atmosphere. There was no support for this project from the institutional power echelons; nursing and housekeeping services objected to the "defacing" of the walls; and the pictures which actually got put up were pulled down (by personnel) within days.

A 1964 prospectus, written by the staff of an institution, contained the following instructions to an architect regarding the design of a new residence building for "trainable retarded adults and young adults:" All interior wall surfaces shall be of a smooth material, and without wall projections other than those specifically stated. All thermostats should be protected with a guard to avoid tampering. Window areas shall be kept consistent with patient needs. Excessive window areas are not desirable. Consideration should be given to using shatterproof glass in patient areas. Door louvers in patient areas should be made of a steel material to withstand patient abuse. Mechanical and electrical equipment and controls throughout the building shall either be tamper-proof or located outside the patient areas. Maximum water temperatures for bath and lavatories must be automatically controlled to eliminate the possibility of scalding. Switches in large patient areas shall be located on the outside of the rooms. A cubicle measuring 24" x 12" x 12" should be provided for each patient." While such instructions are not conclusive evidence that the instructors held the "subhuman" view (rather than some other devaluing view) of residents, such instructions certainly appear to be consistent with such a view.

It cannot be emphasized too strongly that the alleviation of dehumanizing and other undesirable management practices is ultimately more a matter of attitude, rather than of money as widely claimed. There have always been residential facilities that provide exemplary service at very low cost. Usually, such facilities were small, privately operated, and affiliated with religious organizations. On the other hand, one can point to public institutions in the United States where even generous funding and high staff-to-resident ratios have failed to change old practices. Eight attendants can look at 75 residents from behind an unbreakable glass shield as easily as one attendant can, and I have known an institution where this was the sanctioned pattern.

The Retarded Person as a Menace

Unknown events or objects, if alien enough, tend to arouse negative feelings in both man and beast. Man's history consists mostly of his persecution of fellow men who were different in features, skin pigmentation, size, shape, language, customs, dress, etc., and it is apparent that man has been apt to see evil in deviancy. It is not surprising that one role perception prominent in the history of the field is that of the retarded individual as a menace. He/she might be perceived as being a menace individually because of alleged propensities toward various crimes against persons and property; or he/she might be perceived collectively as a social menace because of alleged contribution to social disorganization and genetic decline.

The residential care model derived from the menace perception has much in common with the subhuman model. Certain features, such as segregation from the community, as well as segregation of the sexes, are likely to be accentuated. Since the menace model may ascribe a certain willfulness and evil intent to the retarded individual (in marked contrast to the medical model), an element of vindictiveness and persecution may enter into his management, and some of the protective features of the subhuman model may be omitted. Otherwise, residential features of both models have much in common.

The history of the menace model in the United States will be reviewed later in this essay.

The Retarded Person as an Object of Pity

One residential model is based upon the image of the retarded as objects of pity. Persons possessed of such an image will often hold one or more correlated views:

1. The retarded individual is seen as "suffering" from his condition, and there is emphasis on alleviation of this suffering.
2. Although the person may be seen as "suffering," he may also be believed to be unaware of his deviancy.
3. The retarded person is seen as "an eternal child" who "never grows."
4. Being held blameless for his condition, the person is seen as not accountable for his behavior.
5. The retarded individual is viewed with a "there but for the grace of God go I" attitude.

In residential services, the "pity image" will tend to be expressed in a paternalistic environment which (1) shelters the resident against injury and risk, and (2) which will make few demands for growth, development, and personal responsibility. Both these features may imply infantilization and lack of risks and environmental demands such as stairs, sharp edges, hot water, hot heaters, and electric outlets, as discussed previously.

The pity model has some features in common with the disease and subhuman models. However, there are important differentiating features. The pity model strives to bestow "happiness" upon the retarded person, usually by means of emphasis on programs of fun, religious nurture, and activity for its own sake. This, in turn, is likely to result in allocation of generous space and facilities for music, arts, crafts, parties, picnics, and worship (e.g., a chapel on the grounds).

It is no coincidence that the pity model shares features with the subhuman model: it has many similarities to Vail's (1967) definition of the "man-as-trivium" (i.e., a human being who is not taken seriously or given importance) mode of dehumanization.

The Retarded Person as a Burden of Charity

A person with a strongly moralistic conscience but with little genuine humanism is apt to perceive the retarded as objects of a sour charity. This attitude can best be stereotyped as being that of the Victorian age toward orphans. In colonial America, handicaps were looked upon as the consequence of a stern providence meting out judgment for wickedness. Thus, a natural response to deformity and misfortune might be contempt more than sympathy, and whatever help was rendered was "cold charity" (Deutsch, 1949). The historical roots of state institutions were consistent with this view, since these institutions evolved, in part, from charitable homes for "paupers," orphans, vagrants, etc. (Bartlett, 1967). Even the first institutions for the retarded emphasized admission of children whose parents were unable to provide for their support (see *Journal of Insanity*, 1852, p. 29).

The sour humanist may look upon a retarded resident as a kept object of (public) charity. Charity clients are seen as entitled to food and shelter, but not to anything interpretable as luxuries, frills, and extras. A residence based on this model will be austere and lacking in privacy, individuality, and opportunities to have personal possessions. The resident is expected to be grateful, and to work as much as possible for his "keep." An example of a Victorian "burden of charity" view is found in the following quotation taken from the Massachusetts report at the 1890 National Conference on Charities and Correction: "As to the State schools, it recognizes the value only of such teaching, mental and manual, as shall develop the boy or girl and tend toward a honest and respectable life outside of the institution." "It disapproves of extravagant or luxurious appointments in institutions, as foreign to the spirit of true charity. The inevitable weakening of character by life in institutions, the arrest of development, must be prevented, if possible, by some hardships and privations, such as these boys and girls would be sure to encounter in their own homes or those to which they would be sent" (Reports from States, 1890, p. 329).

Again, much of the physical environment implied by this model will be similar to that of the subhuman model; however, there are certain differentiating architectural and program implications. In a residence built on the charity model, there will be little emphasis upon segregation of residents from the rest of society. There will be a grim and unimaginative emphasis upon eventual self-sufficiency, and while there will be little stress upon environmental enrichment as a means of fostering development, education and training in the traditional handicrafts are likely to be strongly valued.

The Retarded Person as a Holy Innocent

Retarded persons, and possibly those with other handicaps as well, have occasionally been perceived as the special children of God. As such, they are usually seen as incapable of committing evil voluntarily, and consequently may be considered to be living saints. It may also be believed that they have been sent by God for some special purpose.

The role of the retarded as holy or eternal innocents has been recognized in a number of cultures and eras. This role perception was reportedly prevalent among the American Indians, and in medieval Europe. The concept of *"L'enfant du Bon Dieu"* embodies this image.

The holy innocent role has probably had a stronger influence on residential care thinking than is realized—albeit in a subtle way. The holy innocent was generally considered to be harmless, or was indulged much like a child. His presence may even have been valued, as it made the beholder feel a bit closer to heaven and to God. Thus, this role perception tended to *inhibit* the development of specially designated residential facilities, as the innocent were gladly accepted and integrated into the family and the heart of the community. A contemporary example is found in the Hutterite communities in the United States and Canada, studied by Eaton and Weil (1955). In these communities, not one retarded individual had been institutionalized; instead, they were accepted and integrated into the community life.

While the holy innocent perception inhibited the development of special residential placement, it did not prevent it altogether. If residential placement was achieved, however, it tended to be of a very special kind. It might involve placement of the person in a childlike role in a godly home; as a menial worker in religious communities such as monasteries; or as a worker in nursing homes or hospitals run by religious orders. One variant of this practice exists in the Belgian town of Geel where, for centuries, thousands of the mentally handicapped have been boarded in an atmosphere of sheltered benevolence in ordinary homes and have the liberty of the city. The presence of a religious shrine at St. Dymphna—long believed to be (though no longer officially listed as) the patron saint of the mentally afflicted—gave rise to this practice.

Despite its good intentions, the holy innocent model has common elements with a dehumanizing ("man as other") perception described by Vail (1967).

The Retarded Person as a Developing Individual

The developmental model takes an optimistic view of the modifiability of behavior, and usually it does not invest the differentness of the retarded person with strong negative value. Even if severely retarded, he is perceived as capable of growth, development, and learning. The developmental model is characterized by architecture designed to (1) facilitate and encourage the resident's interaction with the environment; (2) maximize interaction between staff and residents; (3) foster individuality, dignity, privacy, and personal responsibility; (4) furnish residents with living conditions which not only permit but encourage functioning similar to that of nonhandicapped community age peers.

In other words, the developmental model provides an atmosphere as similar as possible to that of a typical home, while introducing some additional features which either compensate for handicaps, and/or maximize the likelihood of developmental growth. Administratively, the developmental model will naturally tend to be a decentralized one, in contrast to the medical model, since a resident-oriented atmosphere demands that staff in immediate contact with residents must possess flexibility and freedom to make rapid decisions.

Specific features of the developmental model might include:
(1) Homelike internal and external design.
(2) Colorful, light, bright, perceptually warm but diversified living units.
(3) Small, self-contained living units.
(4) Bedrooms for one or a few residents only.
(5) Family dining facilities.
(6) Homelike appliances such as toilets, faucets, showers, baths, stoves.
(7) Nonstandardization of design and fur-

nishings of living units.
(8) Windows of normal size, type, and placement.
(9) Live-in personnel.
(10) Plenty of space for individual possessions.
(11) Doors between rooms and areas.
(12) Curtains or doors for baths and showers, and toilets designed for private use.
(13) Homelike access to "controls" such as switches and thermostats. The idea here, as with other features, is that potentially objectionable behavior will be modified by interaction with staff, rather than being restricted by the design of the physical environment.
(14) Access to "risks," e.g., stairs, electrical outlets, hot water, etc. Again, the assumption is that residents will be trained to act adaptively, and that controlled risk is part of normal life.

The developmental model implies less of a perception of the retarded as deviant, while striving optimistically to minimize, or compensate for, what differentness there may be. In terms of the old cliche, the retarded are seen as more like, than unlike, others. Although particularly appropriate for children, the developmental model is equally meaningful when applied to adults.

O. R. Lindsley once said that our society is willing to spend money on the design of environments that maintain life, but not on those that maintain dignified behavior. Of all management models, the developmental one is probably most likely to provide the framework for a cathedral of human dignity.

In the early 1900's, a terrible fire in an Ohio facility for the "retarded" caused the institutions across the country to reassess their fire precautions. This fire escape, photographed in 1927 was one institution's response. The design appears to better serve the convenience of the architect than the residents who would need to use the structure in a time of crisis. (1927)

Other Roles of Retarded Persons

In addition to the seven roles discussed above, there are other rather well-defined roles into which the retarded have frequently been cast. For instance, there is the role of the retarded as objects of merriment and ridicule, exemplified in an extreme form in their functioning as court fools and jesters. Though historically prominent, these roles will not be examined further because they have had little effect upon residential models.

THE MEANING OF A BUILDING

That buildings have symbolic qualities is probably universally recognized. This symbolic quality is the meaning referred to here.

Samuel Gridley Howe was probably the most significant and foresighted figure in American history of special education. Through my perusal of original documents, I have formed the conclusion that his role has not yet been fully appreciated, especially vis-a-vis more flamboyant personalities such as Seguin. In 1866, Howe gave the dedication address at the cornerstone-laying of a new institution for the blind in Batavia, New York. By that time, he had been instrumental in founding the early U.S. institutions for both the blind and retarded, had been superintendent of the first such public institution for the retarded (in Massachusetts), and had already perceived and accurately defined most of the shortcomings under which institutions were to labor for the next 100 years. To capture fully the eloquence of Howe's statement on the language of architecture, I have excerpted several passages from his 1866 (pp. 13-16) dedication address:

"Language is of vast extent, and speech is only one of its powers. By speech and by print, men of our generation hold intercourse with each other. There are, moreover, some sorts of language by which the generations of men hold intercourse with other generations, and by which they converse across centuries and cycles of time.

Among the various forms of language between generations, and between the ages, monuments hold a high place.

"As men and women unwittingly, and sometimes unwillingly, reveal their character, and even their secret motives of action, by the sort of language which they use, so the generations unwittingly reveal the prevailing ideas of the men who lived in them, by the works which they leave behind them. Consider the pyramids of Egypt, and read the speech which they utter . . . What say the ten million cubic feet of solid masonry, enclosing two or three small chambers, whose entrances are so narrow that the enclosed sarcophagus must have been placed therein before the walls were built; and those entrances afterwards closed up by huge blocks of stone, too heavy to be moved by any common force? What does all this tell? — What is the language of that generation, spoken by the tongues of the pyramids to this generation?

"It is, that the monarchs were absolute, selfish, cruel and short-sighted. That they built these vast monuments to preserve their fame from oblivion, and their bodies from disturbance . . . The monuments tell us, moreover, that the people must have been ignorant, oppressed, and like 'dumb, driven cattle.'

"They tell us, that great multitudes of men and women were driven in from towns and villages, to toil and moil, and lift stones and carry sand for weeks and months; and when some had died and all were exhausted, then that fresh gangs were driven in to take their places.

"And so of smaller monuments, whether the triumphal arch, where the chained captive walks sadly behind the sculptured conquerors; or the storied column, with its winding procession of battles, assaults and sieges, leading up to the proud victor standing self-glorified on the top. And so of those which tell a better story — the aqueducts, and fountains, the bridges, the canals, the docks and the like.

"If we study the monuments which a generation built, and the kind of men in whose honor they raised statues, we may learn much of the character of the people themselves.

"You are assembled to lay the foundations of a monument which will speak to future generations; and although what you grave upon the cornerstone, and what you put within it, should never be seen, the monument itself will talk to future generations; and what will it tell them?

"It will disclose that the physical condition of the human race in this country was imperfect and unfavorable and that there were born to this generation, and expected to be born in the next, . . . children, numerous enough to form a persistent class. That children of this class were not only loved and cherished by their parents and kindred, but also cared for by the public. That there was no Mount Taygetus here, on which to expose them, with other infirm folk, to perish or be devoured, but asylums into which they were gathered and nurtured.

"It will prove that the social and political union which here leagued three million people into one powerful State, was formed and maintained not only for defense against enemies, for common commercial interest, for great enterprises, for social prosperity and enjoyment, nor yet for mental culture and high civilization of the many, but also for the protection and care of the weak and infirm. That the State of New York, which could dig out a navigable river clear across her broad land, — which had just armed and sent forth three hundred thousand sturdy soldiers to serve the common country and the cause of humanity, — that this great State, while holding on in her high career of material prosperity, and providing schools for all the children, took thought also, that not even the . . . little ones should be neglected.

"In such language will the building, whose foundation-stone you this day lay, speak to many generations in coming time.

"But, while thus noting with pleasure and even excusable pride, the humane impulses which prompt and which will carry forward the work, pardon me if I utter a word of warning.

"Good intentions, and kind impulses do not necessarily lead to wise and truly humane measure.

"Nowhere is wisdom more necessary than in the guidance of charitable impulses. Meaning well is only half our duty; thinking right is the other and equally important half."

A later superintendent from Massachusetts offered an equally relevant insight:

"The history of the development of the human race has been most enduringly written in its architecture. A study of the architecture of a people reveals their dominant thoughts and ideals. The caves of the cave-dweller suggest man's early struggle for existence against wild beasts; the tents of the ancient shepherds reveal the nomadic traits of these people in their moving from place to place in search of food for their flocks. The religious fervor of the middle ages is unmistakably recorded in the cathedral monuments of Europe. The creative and commercial ideals of nations are accurately recorded in their factories, warehouses, docks, highways, and office buildings, and their warlike instincts are well gauged by their forts, armories, battleships, tanks and aeroplanes; their educational interests by their schools and higher seats of learning; their interest in the sick and handicapped are clearly recorded in their hospitals and eleemosynary institutions" (Wallace, 1924, p. 256).

Buildings for the handicapped, like other buildings, can project many meanings. Certain of these meanings are of particular relevance to our discussion. I propose that at least three such relevant meanings can be readily recognized in service facilities: The building as a monument, as a public relations medium, and as a medium of service. Each will be discussed briefly.

The Building as a Monument

Buildings are often erected, consciously or unconsciously, as monuments. In mental retardation facilities, this is especially likely to be true of administration and medical treatment units. The monument may be to a governor; a famous man; a foundation donor, or donor dynasty; or an administrator or professional who may want to achieve identity or "immortality" through this monument-building. Common examples of the latter are the aged superintendent or administrator who wants to make one last, only, or major, contribution before he retires or dies.

While such aspirations often result in genuine benefits to mankind, they can also pervert the consciously verbalized or officially defined purpose of the building. For example, in order to fulfill its function as a monument, the building may be erected in a locality not consistent with optimal program development; available funds may have been so plentiful as to result in a building that is either larger than optimal or over-equipped; limitations of funds may result in a building so small as to require wasteful duplications and adjustments later; the ambitions of the initiator may require a free-standing building where an additional wing or floor on existing buildings would have been preferable; or the concepts which the initiator imposes upon the building plans may force future human services into undesirable and hard-to-remedy patterns. Examples of the latter are donations of facilities such as swimming halls, medical buildings, or churches. The existence of such facilities often makes it very difficult later to establish a pattern of increased use of the community for recreation, medical services, and church attendance. Similarly, an expensive new service building designed to serve large numbers of residents can become a great obstacle to reduction of an institution to a smaller size.

"Let us remember that our purpose is not to build costly monuments, at the expense of the taxpayer, to architects, legislators and governors or indeed to ourselves, . . ." (Kirkbride, 1916, p. 256).

The Building as a Public Relations Medium

A building, or an entire facility, can become a medium of public relations. While such a medium may produce desirable and beneficial results in the long run, the public relations functions may also be irrelevant and even detrimental to the welfare of current residents. A number of examples follow.

1. The building may function as an advertisement for the architect. There are many instances of widely acclaimed buildings which had serious functional shortcomings.

2. Innovations in design may become means of aggrandizement or advancement to staff or superintendents. Real benefits of novel designs may be blown up beyond all proportion. Other widely hailed design innovations may later be recognized as gigantic and foreseeable errors. For example, one institution in the late 1950's erected a new showcase nursery in which the infants' cribs had solid (and expensive) marble sides and wire mesh fronts. Among other things, this obviously could lead to injuries, especially to children with seizures. Only a few years later, the cribs had to be rebuilt at great expense. This was hailed as another dynamic innovation rather than as rectification of a predictable blunder.

3. Finally, a building may be a public relations tool for a governmental or political body. The building may be designed to win votes or good will, to gain power by providing employment opportunities and/or patronage, etc. Again, such buildings may do more harm than good. Erection of large institutions in isolated areas has often been prompted by such public relations (rather than service) considerations.

The Building as a Medium of Service

Finally, buildings may be designed truly and completely with service and function considerations in mind. In residential centers in the United States, such buildings are more likely to be encountered in private rather than public agencies. Too many of our public residential buildings and facilities reflect political, economic, and other considerations which have little to do with resident welfare.

THE FOCUS OF CONVENIENCE OF A BUILDING

Social norms demand that when a residence of some sort is constructed, we must pretend and proclaim that the building is designed for the convenience of the prospective residents. In reality, the building may be designed to serve the convenience of the builder (architect?). If residences are erected with public funds, the convenience of the community can easily become a primary consideration. If the prospective residents belong to a deviant subgroup that requires special management, then the building may be designed for the convenience of the "manager" (who is usually not a resident) rather than the "managed" resident.

The Convenience of the Architect

Some buildings are designed for the convenience of the architectural agent. Such buildings may have required the least imagination, planning, and work from the architect or engineer, while perhaps resulting in the largest profit to him. Many ill-designed, ill-constructed buildings and building complexes bespeak an utter disregard for the prospective resident. However, the building as a monument to the architect, though perhaps well-designed for external beauty and effect, may also fall into the "convenience of the architect" category if resident welfare is neglected.

The Convenience of the Community

The location of a large proportion of institutions in the United States was determined by economic considerations. Institutions were often placed in areas where jobs were needed, and placement became a very political matter. In many instances, institutions were located by the accident of land donations by job-hungry communities. Locations of this nature were not only ill-advised as far as the residents were concerned, but also inconvenient to their families. Furthermore, they resulted in professional and scientific isolation of the staff.

To locate any human service agency with the needs of the server rather than the served in mind is analogous to requiring people to eat in order to provide employment to cooks.

The Convenience of the Staff

Many buildings, when entered, leave little doubt that staff convenience was paramount in the designer's mind. Characteristic elements may include the following:

(1) Caretaker stations providing maximal visual control over resident areas, while minimizing staff involvement; the glass-enclosed nursing station is a classical example.

(2) "Segregated" staff lounges to which staff withdraw for meals, coffee, rest, etc.
(3) Air conditioning for staff, but not for resident areas.
(4) Services such as classrooms, beauty shops, barber shops, and therapy areas that are located in the living units, saving staff the effort of dressing residents or escorting them to other buildings.

The Convenience of the Resident

If built for the welfare and convenience of residents, the location, size, type and internal arrangement of most buildings and institutions in the United States would have been radically different from what they typically have been and are. Again, private facilities appear to have been more apt to be structured with the convenience of residents in mind.

Chapter 2
The Evolution of Institutional Models in the United States

The children, with bowl haircuts and shaven heads, segregated at their tables by sex and color, sit obediently with hands folded and stare attentively at the ongoing activity. These children were decried as the future "degerates" that would threaten the "moral integrity of the race." (1927)

Having discussed certain architectural considerations, and having defined a number of models implicit in various management approaches to the retarded in general and to their residential management specifically, I will now try to trace the residential service models that have been most prominently with us today.

There is a riddle that holds a moral: if fish were intelligent creatures and had scientists and thinkers among them, what would be one of the last things they would probably discover? The answer to the riddle is supposed to be "water." After all, man discovered air only about 300 years ago.

Why do we have institutions at all? Why were they built, and why are they the way they are, and not some other way? Like fish, we have grown up with the fact that institutions exist and that they are places where retarded people are sent. Taking institutions for granted, we have perhaps failed to consider that there are societies that do not have them, or have them in quite a different form than we know.

The last major attempt to interpret rather than merely recount the history of institutions for the retarded in the United States appears to have been made by Davies (1930).[4] His interpretations have been accepted essentially intact by subsequent workers and writers in the field. However, we must consider that as elegant as his interpretations were, they were very close to many historical events he tried to interpret. With another 40 years of perspective behind us, it now seems appropriate to take a fresh look at history, and I will propose some new interpretations or elaborations in an attempt to gain further insight into the nature and origins of our institutional models. Particularly, I will try to demonstrate that attitudes toward deviancy generally have had much to do with the original rise of institutions for the retarded in the United States, and with the way the more common residential models were shaped.

MAKING DEVIANT INDIVIDUALS UNDEVIANT

Around 1850, institutions for a number of deviant groups in the United States were founded for the purpose of making the deviant less deviant. The main means whereby this was to be accomplished was education. In effect, the argument was that deviant persons had to be congregated in one place so that expert and intensive attention could be concentrated on them. I must take issue with the now prevailing notion that the basic aim of the founding figures in our field was essentially and exclusively to reverse ("cure") retardation in children. From reading primary sources, I conclude that the goal was a combination of diminishing the intellectual impairment and increasing adaptive and compensatory skills of pupils so that they would be able to function at least minimally in society.

Wilbur (as quoted in *Journal of Insanity*, 1852, p. 31 ff.) stated:

"We do not propose to create or supply faculties absolutely wanting; nor to bring all grades of idiocy to the same standard of development or discipline; nor to make them all capable of sustaining, creditably, all the relations of a social and moral life; but rather to give to dormant faculties the greatest practicable development, and to apply those awakened faculties to a useful purpose under the control of an aroused and disciplined will.

"But great as are the benefits of education in ordinary cases, its achievements are still greater when, instead of increasing the capacities of the pupils, it substitutes capacities for incapacities; when it restores a class of human beings, now a burden to community, destitute of intelligence, degraded and miserable, to their friends and to society, more capable of development, under the ordinary circumstances of human development; nearer the common standard of humanity, in all respects; more capable of understanding and obeying human laws; of perceiving and yielding to moral obligations; more capable of self-assistance, of self-support, of self-respect, and of obtaining the greatest degree of comfort and happiness with their small means."

The institution was seen as a temporary boarding school. After the child was improved so as to have mastered skills necessary in society, he was to be returned to his family and/or the regular schools. It certainly was not the intent of the pioneers that the institution should become a permanent home. For example, Samuel Gridley Howe said in 1851 of what is now Fernald State School: "This establishment, being intended for a school, should not be converted into an establishment for incurables" (*Journal of Insanity,* 1852, p. 270). "The early teachers of the feebleminded jealously guarded their schools from the danger of becoming asylums. Admission was restricted to those classed as improvables . . . " (Johnson, 1898, p. 465). The institution was seen as " . . . a link in the chain of common schools—the last indeed, but still one necessary in order to make the chain embrace all the children in the state" (Howe, 1852, pp. 15-16). The 1851 bylaws of the first mental retardation institution in New York, opened by Wilbur, are reported to have stated:

"The design and object of the asylum . . . are not of a custodial character but are to furnish all the means of education to that portion of the youth of the state not provided for in any of its other educational institutions . . . Those only will, therefore, be received . . . who are of a proper school attending age, children between the ages of seven and fourteen, who are idiotic and who are not epileptic, insane, nor greatly deformed."

The pioneers also made efforts to distinguish between more and less modifiable retarded persons. Generally, children with symptoms of severe brain injury and with multiple handicaps were not viewed as good prospects (e.g., Howe, 1848; Seguin, 1870). "The most favorable subjects for training, as a general thing, are those who enjoy good bodily health, who are free from epileptic and other fits, and whose heads are not enlarged" (Howe, 1852, p. 12). "The institution is not intended for epileptic or insane children, nor for those who are incurably hydrocephalic or paralytic, and any such will not be retained, to the exclusion of more improvable subjects" (Howe, 1852, p. 36). Seguin, after thirty years' experience, was reported to have said: "Idiots have been improved, educated, and even cured. Not one in a thousand has been entirely refractory to treatment, not one in a hundred who has not been made more happy and healthy. More than 30 per cent. have been taught to conform to moral and social laws, and rendered capable of order, of good feeling, and of working like the third of a man. More than 40 per cent. have become capable of the ordinary transactions of life under friendly control, of understanding moral and social abstractions, or working like two-thirds of a man; and 25 to 30 per cent. have come nearer and nearer the standard of manhood, till some of them will defy the scrutiny of good judges, when compared with ordinary young men and women" (Seguin, as quoted by Carson, 1898, pp. 294-295).

It thus appears that only some retarded children were seen to be proper candidates for institutional education, and this education was to consist mostly of the transformation of poorly socialized, perhaps speechless and uncontrolled children into children who could stand and walk normally, have some speech, eat in an orderly manner, and engage in some kind of meaningful work. It should be kept in mind that perhaps this was equivalent to near-normality in a simpler society than ours today, and that from this fact may have grown the myth of the "curing" hopes of the early pioneers. However, translated to modern conditions, the pioneers appeared to have aspired to not much more than to what our best classes for the severely retarded aspire and frequently accomplish. The pioneers did not so much speak of making "idiots" normal as of "educating the idiot."

The early pioneers held to a number of other ideas and practices of interest to our topic. One of the country's first institutions was privately operated by Wilbur. It was a "school . . . organized on the family plan. The pupils all sat at the same table with the principal, and were constantly under the supervision of some member of the family in the hours of recreation and rest as well as of training." "It was the belief of the managers that only a relatively small number of inmates could be successfully cared for in one institution. It was deemed unwise to congregate a large number of persons suffering from any common infirmity" (Fernald, 1893, p. 206; 209).

"Nearly every one of these early institutions was opened at or near the capitols of their various states, in order that the members of the legislature might closely watch their operation and personally see their need for the results of the instruction and training of these idiots" (Fernald, 1893, p. 209).

Indeed, the institutions were located in the very hearts of the community. The first public institution in the United States, established in Massachusetts by an 1848 act, was located for a time in a large rented residence in South Boston (*Journal of Insanity,* 1852, p. 27) " . . . in a crowded neighborhood" (Kerlin, 1885, p. 159).[5] Shortly thereafter, the first public institution of the State of New York was located in a " . . . large, spacious, airy, well arranged building on the Troy road, about two miles from the capitol . . . " (*Journal of Insanity,* 1852, p. 28). This building, too, was rented.

The rationale that the retarded can be and should be removed from society in order to be trained for return to society, though of very questionable validity, is still alive today. We can still see this rationale implemented today, as when groups of retarded adults are placed in an institution for six months of training under some federal grant. However, it should be noted that the basic rationale for segregating deviant individuals for behavioral reshaping not only lacks adequate empirical foundation, but is actually contrary to a vast store of empirical findings.

Essentially, making the deviant person undeviant implied a developmental model. Furthermore, residential schooling was seen not merely as a privilege or worthy charity, but a right of the retarded and a duty of society. Again, Howe (1848, pp. 52-54) was a hundred years ahead of his time, and perhaps decades ahead of some of our contemporaries.

" . . . the immediate adoption of proper means of training and teaching idiots, may be urged upon higher grounds than that of expediency, or even of charity; it may be urged upon the ground of imperative duty. It has been shown, that the number of this wretched class is fearfully great, that a large part of them are directly at the public charge; that the whole of them are at the charge of the community in one way or another, because they cannot help themselves. It has been shown, that they are not only neglected, but that, through ignorance, they are often badly treated, and cruelly wronged; that, for want of proper means of training, some of them sink from mere weakness of mind, into entire idiocy so that, though born with a spark of intellect which might be nurtured into a flame, it is gradually extinguished, and they go down darkling to the grave, like the beasts that perish. Other countries are beginning to save such persons from their dreadful fate; and it must not longer be, that here, in the home of the Pilgrims, human beings, born with some sense, are allowed to sink into hopeless idiocy, for want of a helping hand.

"Massachusetts admits the right of all her citizens to a share in the blessings of education, and she provides it liberally for all her more favored children. If some be blind or deaf, she still continues to furnish them with special instruction at great cost; and will she longer neglect the poor idiot, — the most wretched of all who are born to her, — those who are usually abandoned by their fellows, — who can never, of themselves, step up upon the platform of humanity, — will she leave them to their dreadful fate, to a life of brutishness, without an effort in their behalf?

"It is true, that the plea of ignorance can be made in excuse for the neglect and ill-treatment which they have hitherto received; but this plea can avail us no longer. Other countries have shown us that idiots may be trained to habits of industry, cleanliness, and self-respect; that the highest of them may be measurably restored to self-control, and that the very lowest of them may be raised up from the slough of animal pollution in which they wallow; and can the men of other countries do more than we? Shall we, who can transmute granite and ice into gold and silver, and think it pleasant work, — shall we shrink from the higher task of transforming brutish men back into human shape? Other countries are beginning to rescue their idiots from further deterioration, and even to elevate them; and shall our Commonwealth continue to bury the humble talent of lowly children committed to her motherly care, and let it rot in the earth, or shall she do all that can be done, to render it back with usury to Him who let it? There should be no doubt about the answer to these questions. The humanity and justice of our rulers will prompt them to take immediate measures for the formation of a school or schools for the instruction and training of idiots.

"The benefits to be derived from the establishment of a school for this class of persons, upon humane and scientific principles, would be very great. The school, if conducted by persons of skill and ability, would be a model for others . . . it would be demonstrated that no idiot need be confined or restrained by force; that the young can be trained to industry, order, and self-respect; that they can be redeemed from odious and filthy habits, and that there is not one of any age, who may not be made more of a man, and less of a brute, by patience and kindness, directed by energy and skill." "Now, we claim for idiots a place in the human family" (p. 17).

As the foregoing quotation and the one following below illustrate, the founding of the early institutions was accompanied by a pride, hope, and euphoria we can scarcely comprehend: "Let us now turn to the present: like Rome, we Americans can also boast of God-like men in our annals, and illustrious deeds on the historic page; as she had, we likewise are perhaps characterized by prominent faults, and by some compensating virtues." "Our eagles too have flown over a space equal to that which was traversed by those of Rome. To the Obelisks, and especially to the Cyclopean Coliseum we can show nothing equal or analogous. But we possess a class of institution scattered throughout our country, to which Rome was a stranger, and through which we have attained an exalted position that she never reached, or even had the soul to aspire unto" (attributed to an 1859 superintendent by DeProspo, 1966, p. 37).

PROTECTING DEVIANT INDIVIDUALS FROM NONDEVIANT PEOPLE

As mentioned earlier, history appears to have wronged the founding fathers in ascribing to them the hope of "curing" large numbers of the retarded. Our texts also seem to be partially mistaken in judging the early institutions to have failed to reach their objectives. Many residents *were* much improved under the tight and well-planned training regimens of the pioneers, and a substantial proportion of trainees did, indeed, return to the community.

About 26 per cent of residents discharged in Connecticut were believed to be self-supporting (Knight, 1879). In Kentucky, in 1884 alone, about 3 per cent of the residents of the state institution were placed into community employment (Kerlin, 1885, p. 166), and about 19 per cent of all new admissions were eventually discharged as self-supporting (Rogers, 1888, pp. 102-103). "The experience of the past thirty years proves that, of those who are received and trained in institutions, 10 to 20 per cent are so improved as to be able to enter life as breadwinners; that from 30 to 40 per cent are returned to their families so improved as to be self-helpful, or at least much less burdensome to their people;" (Kerlin, 1888, p. 100). At Glenwood (Iowa), 68 of 195 residents were separated between 1885 and 1887, and 10 to 20 per cent of the residents appeared to attain eventual self-sufficiency in the community (Powell, 1887). "All of our schools for the feeble-minded have succeeded in sending out a goodly number of persons who are bearing bravely their share of the burden of life" (Rogers, 1888, p. 102).

There were, however, four problems:

1. There were bound to be failures with a certain proportion of residents.

2. For every resident successfully discharged, the statistical probabilities (due to the law of re-

gression) were that his replacement would be less successful. It is hard to improve upon successful habilitation; it is much easier to fail thereafter.

3. Many residents who could have been partially habilitated had no place to return to, and thus, after some years, their continued presence reduced turnover. Seguin referred to this as early as 1870 as a "... paternal, not yet legalized, arrangement" (p. 12), and Fernald (1893, p. 210) later described it as follows: "In the course of a few years, in the annual reports of these institutions we find the superintendents regretting that it was not expedient to return to the community a certain number of the cases who had received all the instruction the school had to offer." "It was found that only a small proportion ... could be so developed and improved that they could go out into the world and support themselves independently. A large number, as a result of the school discipline and training, could be taken home where they became comparatively harmless and unobjectionable members of the family, capable, and under the loving and watchful care of their friends, of earning by their labor as much as it cost to maintain them. But in many cases the guardians of these children were unwilling to remove them from the institution, and begged that they might be allowed to remain where they could be made happy and kept from harm. Many of these cases were homeless and friendless, and, if sent away from the school, could only be transferred to almshouses where they became depraved and demoralized by association with adult paupers and vagrants of both sexes. It was neither wise nor humane to turn these boys and girls out to shift for themselves. The placing of these feeble-minded persons always proved unsatisfactory. Even those who had suitable homes and friends able and willing to become responsible for them, by the death of these relatives were thrown on their own resources and drifted into pauperism and crime. It gradually became evident that a certain number of these higher-grade cases needed life-long care and supervision, and that there was no suitable provision for this permanent custody outside these special institutions."

4. Many people, as evident in our textbooks, had misunderstood the objectives of the pioneers in expecting complete and rapid cures in large numbers, and interpreted any lesser accomplishment as tantamount to failure.

At any rate, with the perceived failure of the institution as a school, and the inability of many adult residents to adjust to the community, ideologies changed between about 1870 and 1880. Developmental attitudes degenerated into pity and charity, and as they did, the residential model changed from a developmental one to a pity model. The idea grew that the retarded should be viewed as innocent victims of fate or parental sin, and that instead of schooling, loving care and protection should be bestowed upon them.

"In the race of life, where an individual who is backward or peculiar attempts to compete with those who are not, the disadvantages are so great that the graduate from the idiot asylum really has no chance to succeed. The capacity of the individual is not at fault; but the world is not full of philanthropic people who are willing to take the individual from the asylum and surround him with the proper guardianship which his case demands" (C. T. Wilbur, 1888, p. 110).

The term "school" began to disappear from the names of institutions, being replaced by the term "asylum." For example, in 1893, the "Custodial Asylum for Unteachable Idiots" was founded at Rome, New York. "Give them an asylum, with good and kind treatment; but not a school." "A well-fed, well-cared for idiot, is a happy creature. An idiot awakened to his condition is a miserable one" (Governor Butler of Massachusetts, 1883, as quoted by Rogers, 1898, pp. 152-153). "It is earnestly urged that the best disposal to be made of this large class of the permanently disabled is to place it in custodial departments of institutions for the feeble-minded persons, in buildings judiciously remote from the educational and industrial departments, but under the same merciful system that inspires hope and help for the lowest of humanity, and under a broadly classified administration that will admit of the employment of the so-called moral idiot, thereby diminishing greatly the burden to the charitable and the taxpayer" (Kerlin, 1888, p. 100). "The question of unimprovability then being once established, the only practicable thing to do is to furnish a home where, amid cheerful surroundings, in accordance with the state of our Christian civilization, and in a manner consistent with an age of practical economy, the mediocre imbecile may lead a happy, harmless, and measurably useful life in assisting to care for his fellows" (Rogers, 1888, p. 103). "They must be kept quietly, safely, away from the world, living like the angels in heaven, neither marrying nor given in marriage" (Johnson, 1889, p. 319).

"Institutions have changed their character, largely to furnish a permanent residence with congenial surroundings for these unfortunates" (Wilmarth, 1902, p. 157). Illinois erected a "hospital building" for custodial purposes in 1885; a custodial department was installed in Iowa the same year; Connecticut made its first appropriation for such a building that year; and Pennsylvania built such a building in 1886 (Kerlin, 1886, pp. 289-294).

The Institution was no longer to be a school, but a shelter, an asylum of happiness, a garden of Eden for the innocent. What doubt there may have remained was largely dispelled by the close of the century: "Slowly but surely the conviction has become general, especially among the trustees and officers of institutions, that admission as a pupil of the training school should be but the first step to permanent care; that, with a few exceptions, so few that they may be disregarded in establishing a policy, all the pupils of the school, from the lowest to the highest grade, ought to be permanently retained in the safe, kindly, maternal care of the state. The above conviction is held by all who have expressed themselves publicly within the last few years in this country, excepting a few persons whose pecuniary interests seem in conflict with such a theory. It has been acted upon by the legislature of many states, whose laws have been changed by removing from the institution code the age limit of retention, and in some cases of acceptance." "A belief in the necessity of permanent care of all this defective class is professed by the superintendent of every state school for the feebleminded in the United States" (Johnson, 1898, p. 467).

The protective residential model emphasized benevolent shelter, but it bore the seeds of three dangerous trends: (1) isolation, (2) enlargement, and (3) economization.

1. The retarded person was to be moved out of society, in order to spare him the stresses he was believed incapable of bearing, and to provide him with protection from the persecution and ridicule of the nondeviant. The idea that the retarded must be protected from society, rather than vice versa, was well expressed by Kerlin (1884, p. 260): "The general grounds of the institution should be hedged or fenced to keep off improper intrusion but be freely used by the inmates for walking exercise and work." H. B. Wilbur (1879, p. 96) recommended that institution grounds be fenced " . . . for the privacy of the inmates." Thus, institutions began to be removed from population centers and located in pastoral surroundings.

Writers of the period waxed rhapsodic over their own benevolence and drew an idyllic picture of the new trend: " . . . Here and there, scattered over the country, may be 'villages of the simple,' made up of the warped, twisted, and the incorrigible, happily contributing to their own and the support of those more lowly, — 'cities of refuge,' in truth; havens in which all shall live contentedly, because no longer misunderstood nor taxed with extractions beyond their mental or moral capacity" (Kerlin, 1885, p. 174). " . . . God's innocent ones . . . " (Kerlin, 1886, p. 288) were to reside " . . . in harmony with the spirit of a progressive age and a Christian philanthropy" (Rogers, 1888, p. 105) in " . . . noble institutions of the times—those temples sacred to the restoration of fallen humanity, nearer Christ in His work than half the shrines dedicated in His name . . . " (Greene, 1884, p. 269). These institutions were being " . . . sustained . . . by an abounding popular sympathy . . . " (Kerlin, 1886, p. 291) and were " . . . supplementing the work of the Creator" (Pickett, 1885, p. 449).

If the institution was to be a Garden of Eden, it needed lands and gardens, and sure enough, an emphasis on gardening and farming developed. Thus, Osborne (1891) stated: "Ample acreage (not less than one acre per patient) will be provided for the proper seclusion of defectives from the stare of the idle and curious . . . " Kerlin (1884, p. 165) described the Connecticut institution as being " . . . beautifully situated on a large farm . . ", and by 1915, Schlapp (1915, p. 322) was able to say: "Most of our institutions are beautifully situated in the country." To this day, the phrase "happy farm" (much like "funny farm") is occasionally heard in reference to state hospitals and institutions for the retarded.

2. The idea developed that if there was to be special protective care, it would be advantageous to congregate larger numbers of residents together. If institutions had to serve both an educational and custodial function, and if, for several decades, the educational department of an institution turned over more graduates to the custodial department than the latter discharged (usually because of death), then it followed that institutions were under multiple pressure to grow. And grow they did. For instance, in Massachusetts, the first call by the trustees for substantial enlarging of the institution came in 1881, and this enlargement was to accommodate not only the "improvables" but also the "unimprovables" (Kerlin, 1885a, p.159). In Ohio, the transition from the smaller educational to the larger custodial institution was aided greatly by a disastrous fire in the year 1881. "Perhaps no trouble weighed more heavily upon the management than an effort to prevent the reconstruction of the building as an educational institution for feeble-minded children." The issue was "squarely met," and $400,000 was appropriated to construct the " . . . best built and the best appointed institution in the world . . . " — for 600 residents (Kerlin, 1885a, pp. 163-164).

It is fascinating to trace the enlargement of institutions, and the fitful process of rationalization that accompanied it. First, to make room for rationalizing the enlargement, the pioneers' ideal of the small institution had to be destroyed. Paradoxically, this was done by accusing small institutions of 'hospitalism': "It is the small institution against which may be pronounced the objection of moral hospitalism. The large, diffuse, and thoroughly classified institution is another affair, and can be to its wards and employees as cosmopolitan as a city" (Kerlin, 1884, p. 262). "The growth of our institution to the proportion of a village, as earnestly urged by the superintendent, divides the board. The conservative element, which from the beginning has considered an institution of fifty or sixty children as the ideal, is still struggling against the inevitable. But thanks to Ohio, which continues to show us the way, in which all progressive States will follow" (Kerlin, 1885b, p. 369).

As usual, the irresistible trend toward enlargement was, at first, rationalized as being for the benefit of the resident. One detects the sentiment, present perhaps in all generations, that it is better for the deviant if they associate with their own kind: "We find that we must congregate them to get our best results. It is only from a large number that we can select enough of any one grade to make a group or class." "In order to have companionship, the most necessary thing in the education of all children, we must have large numbers from which to make up our small classes of those who are of an equal degree of intelligence" (Knight, 1891, p. 108). "We have also proved that we must have *large* institutions if we would get the best results; for, while the training of the imbecile must always depend mainly upon individual effort, yet the types are so diverse that it is only from considerable numbers that classes of a general degree of development are secured" (Knight, 1895, p. 153). "I believe that a large state institution is the best place for the feeble-minded or idiotic child" (Johnson, 1901, p. 410).

Others were more candid and advocated enlargement as a means of reducing cost, and during the pity period, the first arguments for the need of inexpensive care were heard. Wilbur had warned in 1880: "It will be readily seen that the cost of maintenance in such an establishment is a more important one than in the case of the educational institutions" (as quoted by Kerlin, 1885, p. 161). In about 1887, an act was passed in Pennsylvania which raised the number of state-supported residents from 400 to 500 while reducing the permissible per capita expenditure from $200 to $175 (Kerlin, 1888). "We have proved too, that in large institutions we can give employment to those adult imbeciles who are beyond what we call the 'school age' . . . As superintendents of institutions we are working out new methods in management, in economy and education . . ." (Knight, 1895, p. 561).

Rogers, in 1888 (p. 106), took one last look over his shoulders, as he and the field plunged ahead: " . . . to those who fear the growth of large and unwieldy institutions we only say that matters of that kind must be settled by the communities which are responsible for them. If this danger appears, stop the growth and build another institution, but do not warp the usefulness of any by a narrow comprehension of its functions."

By 1893, Fernald (p. 215) had observed a phenomenon familiar to us all: "Successive legislatures have been ready to enlarge existing institutions when they would not grant appropriations for establishing new ones." Thus, institutions changed from small intimate homes, for children counted in the dozens, to huge facilities for thousands of residents, and in 1893, Fernald could already refer to institutions as " . . . these immense households" (p. 218).

3. Initially, as a constructive substitute for educational activities, increasing emphasis was placed on the work of the residents. Purportedly, the work was " . . . not for the value of the work itself, but for its value to the child" (Kerlin, 1885, p. 162). "The work-shop where several such industries are carried on provides occupation and relief from the depressing ennui of idleness, and at the same time fosters physical development and intellectual growth" (quoted from a Massachusetts report by Kerlin, 1885, p. 159). "With their daily tasks, their feeble minds directed, the time taken up in work or exercise, their days are spent in safety, pleasantness, and peace" (First Annual Report of the Trustees of the New York State Custodial Asylum for Feebleminded Women, as quoted by Kerlin, 1886, p. 290), " . . . the farm thus serving to provide healthful and attractive occupation for the stronger members of the institution . . . " (Reports from States, 1896, p. 37).

As usual, however, noble sentiments gave way to utilitarian practices, and the economic value of work to the institution began to be stressed: " . . . the trained capacities of the stronger shall be made available for the aid of the weaker and for the diminution of public charge" (Kerlin, 1886, p. 269).

The economic emphasis, in the rural America of about 1880, implied adoption of agricultural pursuits, which, in turn, required land. The trend toward farming, combined with the desire to protect the retarded, resulted in locating institutions in isolated rural areas. For instance, establishment of the first farm colony (the "Howe Farm") in Massachusetts in 1881 (Kerlin, 1885; Fernald, 1902) became the occasion for moving residents from the institution in the heart of Boston out into the country, and to the periphery of society. Kansas opened its first state institution in 1881 near Lawrence, seat of the University, and Leavenworth, one of the important crossroads of the West. Three years later, the institution was moved far away onto a farm near Winfield (Kerlin, 1885, p. 169; Status of the Work, 1886, p. 451) because the land had been donated, and in order to deal a blow to the University.

Vail (1967) has classified the pity attitude as a special and subtle type of dehumanization. This may have been very insightful, since once the developmental attitude changed to pity, pity lasted only about 10-20 years, and was followed by a long period of brutalization. In our society, pity is usually extended to a person who is perceived as suffering. However, much of suffering, as we conceptualize it, implies that the sufferer should receive some kind of help, which may consume the time, money, emotional involvement or efforts of others. Suffering, by its very nature, thus

Pear picking was one activity pursued in this so-called farm colony. It was the hope of the institution that with sufficient farm land " . . . able bodied imbeciles of both sexes could be kept in our state at a weekly cost of not more than $1 per capita in addition to what the farm would produce." (1925)

makes a demand on a conscience developed in the Judeo-Christian tradition. This demand, in turn, may create resentment, especially if the sufferer does not "get well," and resentment may lead to brutalization. The fact that one of the most influential social organizations between 1874 and 1917 was the National Conference on Charities and Correction is of relevance, as it shows that the bestowers of pity and the controllers of menace had great commonalities.

PROTECTING NONDEVIANT INDIVIDUALS FROM THE DEVIANT PEOPLE

Preceding and paralleling the education and pity periods, there had existed a current of negative attitudes toward the retarded. These attitudes, the three dangerous trends mentioned in the last section, and a new conceptualization of the retarded, combined to shape a new institutional model which is essentially the model embodied in most of our large, public institutions today.

The Early Indictment

The image of the retarded as a social menace grew in a subtle way. As early as the mid 1880's, the alarm was sounded: "But the State, adopting as its policy the protection in institutions of the defective classes, acquires a right of inquest into the causes generating this tremendous burden to the thrifty tax-payer, who must be protected from the rapacious social ills which deplete his own strength" (Kerlin, 1884, p. 262). An early president of the National Conference on Charities and Correction was later quoted by Wilmarth (1902, p. 160) as having said: "'My child, your life has been one succession of failures. You cannot feed and clothe yourself honestly: you cannot control your appetites and passions. Left to yourself, you are not only useless, but mischievous. Henceforth I shall care for you.'" "Is there anything more worthy the thoughtful attention of the statesmen of our land than to improve our methods of *support* of the weak ones so that we may add to it the needed element 'control?'" (Johnson, 1903, p. 252).

" . . . Can it be deemed wise, either for society or the defective himself, to turn him loose after some years of training to make his fight for existence on his own behalf?" "No amount of moral training during his school life can render him capable of judging points of morality for himself or make him proof against temptations to which his natural tendencies incline him to yield. The end will almost inevitably be that he will drift back into the care of the state, but through the gates of crime" (Dunphy, 1908, p. 331). "What in the beginning was a philanthropic purpose, *pure* and *simple,* having for its object the most needy, and therefore naturally directed toward paupers and idiots, now assumes the proportions of socialistic reform as a matter of self-preservation, a necessity to preserve the nation from the encroachments of imbecility, of crime, and all the fateful consequences of a highly nervous age" (Barr, 1899, p. 208).

Fernald (1915, pp. 289-290) summarized the trend as follows: "During the last decade four factors have materially changed the professional and popular conception of the problem of the feeble-minded.

1. The widespread use of mental tests has greatly simplified the preliminary recognition of ordinary cases of mental defect and done much to popularize the knowledge of the extent and importance of feeble-mindedness.

2. The intensive studies of the family histories of large numbers of the feeble-minded by Goddard, Davenport, and Tredgold have demonstrated what had hitherto only been suspected, that the great majority of these persons are feeble-minded because they come from family stocks which transmit feeble-mindedness from generation to generation in accordance with the laws of heredity. Many of the members of these families are not defective, themselves, but these normal members of tainted families are liable to have a certain

number of defectives among their own descendants. The number of persons who are feeble-minded as a result of injury, disease, or other environmental conditions without hereditary predisposition is much smaller than had been suspected, and these accidental cases do not transmit their defect to their progeny.

3. The cumulative evidence furnished by surveys, community studies, and intensive group inquiries have now definitely proved that feeble-mindedness is an important factor as a cause of juvenile vice and delinquency, adult crime, sex immorality, the spread of venereal disease, prostitution, illegitimacy, vagrancy, pauperism, and other forms of social evil and social disease.

4. Our estimates of the extent and the prevalence of feeble-mindedness have been greatly increased by the application of mental tests, the public school classes for defectives, and interpretation of the above-mentioned antisocial expressions of feeble-mindedness, and the intensive community studies. Goddard believes that at least 2 per cent of school children in the first five grades are mentally defective. It is conservative to say that there are at least four feeble-minded persons to each thousand of the general population.

There are reasons for believing that feeble-mindedness is on the increase, that it has leaped its barriers, so to speak, as a result of changed conditions of civilization" (Fernald, 1915, pp. 289-290).

One might add here that a fifth point was the belief that the retarded were reproducing at a more prolific rate than the nonretarded, and might therefore "outbreed" the latter.

The Peak of the Indictment

As time passed, the social indictment of the retarded grew more direct, severe, and shrill. Barr said: "Of all dependent classes there are none that drain so entirely the social and financial life of the body politic as the imbecile, unless it be its close associate, the epileptic" (1902, p. 163). Butler (1907, p. 10) added: "While there are many anti-social forces, I believe none demands more earnest thought, more immediate action than this. Feeble-mindedness produces more pauperism, degeneracy and crime than any other one force. It touches every form of charitable activity. It is felt in every part of our land. It affects in some way all our people. Its cost is beyond our comprehension."

"When we view the number of the feeble-minded, their fecundity, their lack of control, the menace they are, the degradation they cause, the degeneracy they perpetuate, the suffering and misery and crime they spread, — these are the burden we must bear" (Butler, 1915, p. 361). "For many generations we have recognized and pitied the idiot. Of late we have recognized a higher type of defective, the moron, and have discovered that he is a burden; that he is a menace of society and civilization; that he is responsible to a large degree for many, if not all, of our social problems" (Goddard, 1915, p. 307). " . . . We preach . . . that . . . the feeble-minded at large unguarded are a menace to the community" (Cornell, 1915, p. 322). " . . . Those unfortunate members of society who fall so far short of the line of normal mentality as to be an inherent social menace." " . . . It is among this group that there flourishes the real peril to the mental and moral stamina of our nation." "The problem itself is the most serious facing the country today" (Schlapp, 1915, pp. 320-321).

Bullard (1910, pp. 14-15), in the strongest statement of indictment of retarded women, warned: "Girls of the classes described must be cared for by the state . . . There is no class of persons in our whole population who, unit for unit, are so dangerous or so expensive to the state. This excepts no class, not even the violently insane. They are much more dangerous and expensive than the ordinary insane or the ordinary feeble-minded or the ordinary male criminal." He (1910, p. 320) added: "There is probably no class of persons who are more fitted and more apt to spread disease and moral evil than these girls," and "One evil girl may corrupt a whole village." "A single feeble-minded girl among a group of young boys becomes a plague-spot, the consequences of which are frightful" (Butler, 1915, p. 358).

It can be noted from the statements quoted above that while retarded males were seen as a "menace of the greatest magnitude," females were seen as even more dangerous, if this is possible: "It is certain that the feeble-minded girl or woman in the city rarely escapes the sexual experiences that too often result in the birth of more defectives and degenerates" (Fernald, 1912, p. 90). " . . . Imbecile girls and women everywhere are an easy prey to the wiles and lust of brutal men, . . . " (Carson, 1898, p. 296). "Few of these girls permanently escape, unless they are specially cared for by wise and understanding people. Their care demands unceasing vigilance and constant thought, which can rarely be properly exercised outside of an institution. As a fact, these girls—unless cared for permanently in an institution—usually become immoral or are led away to make bad marriages. In either case their children are apt to be mentally defective, with more or less pronounced animal instincts, diseased and depraved, a curse and menace to the community. This goes on constantly increasing unless we take means . . . to prevent the production of children. The evil that one feeble-minded woman can cause through the production of feeble-minded children is incalculable. It has often been plainly stated: statistics have been carefully compiled and the results are too well known to need repetition before this Conference" (Bullard, 1910, pp. 333-334). "Feeble-minded women are almost invariably immoral, and if at large usually become carriers of venereal disease or give birth to children who are as defective as themselves. The feeble-minded woman who marries is twice as prolific as the normal woman" (Fernald, 1912, pp. 90-91). Schlapp (1915, p. 323) referred to " . . . the feeble-minded pregnant woman who is, naturally unmoral." "The debasing and demoralizing influence of an unrestrained feeble-minded woman in a community is beyond the comprehension of the uniformed" (Butler, 1907, p. 2).

Fernald was one of the strongest indictors: "And pauperism breeding other paupers, what is it but imbecility let free to do its mischief?" "The tendency to lead dissolute lives is especially noticeable in the females. A feeble-minded girl is exposed as no other girl in the world is exposed" (Fernald, 1893, p. 212). Later, (1904, p. 383) he said: "It is well known that feeble-minded women and girls are very liable to become sources of unspeakable debauchery and licentiousness which pollutes the whole life of the young boys and youth of the community. They frequently disseminate in a wholesale way the most loathsome and deadly diseases, permanently poisoning the minds and bodies of thoughtless youth at the very threshold of manhood. Almost every country town has one or more of these defective women each having from one to four or more illegitimate children, every one of whom is predestined to be defective mentally, criminal, or an outcast of some sort.

"The modern American community is very intolerant of the presence of these dangerous defectives with the desires and passions of adult life, without control of reason and judgment. There is a widespread and insistent demand that these women be put under control" (Fernald, 1904, p. 383). "The adult males become the town loafers and incapables, the irresponsible pests of the neighborhood, petty thieves, purposeless destroyers of property, incendiaries, and very frequently violators of women and little girls" (Fernald, 1904, p. 383). "The social and economic burdens of uncomplicated feeble-mindedness are only too well known. The feeble-minded are a parasitic, predatory class, never capable of self-support or of managing their own affairs. The great majority ultimately become public charges in some form. They cause considerable sorrow at home and are a menace and danger to the community." "Every feeble-minded person, especially the high-grade imbecile, is a potential criminal, needing expression of his criminal tendencies. The unrecognized imbecile is a most dangerous element in the community." "It has been truly said that feeble-mindedness is the mother of crime, pauperism and degeneracy. It is certain that the feeble-minded and the progeny of the feeble-minded constitute one of the great social and economic burdens of modern times" (Fernald, 1912, p. 90; 91; 92).

The peak of the indictment of the retarded was reached between 1908 and 1915, and was embodied in three important documents:

1. The 1908 British Royal Commission Report, which became very influential: "The evidence points unmistakenly to the fact that mentally defective children often have immoral tendencies; that they are greatly lacking in self-control; and moreover are peculiarly open to suggestion, so that they are at the mercy of bad companions."

"Many competent observers are of the opinion that if the constantly or recurring fatuous and irresponsible crimes and offenses of mentally defective persons are to be prevented, long and continuous detention is necessary. The experience of the prison authorities fully confirms this opinion. From the earliest age, when they appear before the magistrates as children on remand or as juvenile offenders, until and throughout the adult period of their lives, the mentally defective, at first reprimanded and returned to their parents, then convicted and subjected to a short sentence and returned to their parents, and then later continually sentenced and resentenced and returned to their parents or friends until, for crimes of greater gravity, they pass through the convict prisons, are treated, as this reiterated evidence shows, without hope and without purpose, and in such a way as to allow a feeble-minded progeny which may become criminal like themselves. This, as has been said, is an 'evil of the very greatest magnitude.' The absolute and urgent necessity of coping with it is undeniable" (Royal Commission Report of 1908, quoted in Davies, 1923).

2. Fernald (1912) wrote a damning indictment of the retarded in his famous address on "The Burden of Feeble-Mindedness," a burden he had earlier (1893, p. 213) called "disgusting."

3. Bullard (1910) wrote an incredible diatribe about the particular immorality and menace of retarded women.

In weighing the influence of some of the indictors quoted in preceding and subsequent sections, let the reader be reminded that the following 25 persons had been, or became, presidents of what is now the American Association on Mental Deficiency: C. T. Wilbur, Stewart, Powell, Fish, G. H. Knight, Carson, Rogers, Kerlin, Osborne, Wilmarth, Barr, Dunlap, Johnson, Polglase, Murdoch, Smith, Bullard, Goddard, Emerick, Watkins, and Anderson; Bernstein, Fernald, Johnstone, and Wallace held the presidency twice. Johnson had also been president of the National Conference on Charities and Correction, as well as its general secretary for many years. This latter organization was perhaps the major vehicle of the indictment, since it was a major forum for indictment speeches and papers, and since it encompassed those professionals most intimately concerned with social processes, such as social workers, sociologists, legal and law enforcement personnel, psychiatrists, psychologists, public health and immigration workers, and officials from all levels of government.

Dehumanizing and Brutalizing Elements of the Indictment

The indictment contained some ominous notes. Streeter (1915, p. 340) said: " . . . in feeble-mindedness lies the tap root of most of our social problems; the only effective radical way to deal with these problems, is to strike at this tap root with the strong ax of prevention." Barr (1902a; 1902b), a very influential past president of what is now the American Association on Mental Deficiency, issued an "Imperative Call of Our Present to Our Future," followed by an address entitled "The Imbecile and Epileptic *Versus* the Taxpayer and the Community." The title of a book by Crookshank in 1924 was enough to drive a shudder down anyone's spine: "The Mongol in Our Midst."

Where we, today, speak of combatting mental retardation, as in the President's Panel "National

Plan To Combat Mental Retardation," phrases with menacing overtones were used in the alarmist period, as when Johnson (1898, p. 471) spoke of "stamping out" idiocy and imbecility. That this was more than a figure of speech became clear 2 years later, when he stated: "I do not think that, to prevent the propagation of this class it is necessary to kill them off or to resort to the knife; but, if it is necessary, it should be done" (Johnson, 1901, pp. 410-411). Alexander Johnson, past president of the National Conference of Charities and Correction, and of what is now the American Association on Mental Deficiency, was one of the most influential figures in the social action field of the era.

One gentleman from Massachusetts, in 1885, was reported to have called for the same solution to the problem of feeble-mindedness as that which had been "applied theoretically and also practically to the Indian question" (*Conference on Charities and Correction,* 1888, p. 396), and Taft (1918, p. 545) ominously referred to a " . . . final . . . solution . . . ", a term that would come into its full meaning 20 years later.

In any society that places high value on intelligence and achievement, there is probably a predisposition to brutalize and dehumanize the inadequate deviant person. When the deviant person is seen as not only inadequate but also as a menace, latent dehumanization becomes overt. It therefore should not surprise us that during the alarmist period, the retarded were dehumanized in both word and deed.

Analogies based on examples from the animal, vegetable, and mineral world are sometimes offered to explain a point about retardation. Such analogies are ill-chosen at best; at worst, they reveal that the person using such an analogy perceives the retarded as subhuman. Some examples of ill-chosen word pictures used during the indictment period follow. Kerlin (1884, p. 249) said of a retarded person: "With his great luminous soft, jet eyes, he reminds one of a seal." Fernald (1915, p. 291) observed: "We now have state commissions for controlling the gypsy moth and boll weevil, the foot-and-mouth disease, and for protecting the shell-fish and wild game, but we have no commission which even attempts to modify or control the vast social, moral and economic forces represented by the feeble-minded persons at large in the community." Davenport (quoted by Fernald, 1915, p. 290) moved from "unfit animal strains" to "weak strains" to the "feeble-minded" in the space of two sentences.

Simultaneous reference to animal breeding and to reproduction of the retarded abounded. Brewer (1895, p. 467) referred to the retarded as " . . . this breed of men" being a " . . . poor breed of stock." Barr (1902, p. 163) had this to say: "We are very careful as to the breeding, inbreeding, or non-breeding of our flocks and herds and beasts of burden; but we allow epileptics and irresponsible imbeciles to taint pure stock or to reproduce their kind unmolested without intervention." The important role of a national association of cattlemen in the study of prevention of retardation is noteworthy and will be touched upon again later in this essay. Wines (1889, p. 321; also quoted by Bicknell, 1896) said about retarded workers: "Many of them are capable of being made useful to a large extent even though they may be unable to talk. I have seen idiots who were useful on a farm, for instance, who could not speak a word. Is not a mule valuable on a farm? Yet he cannot talk." One might have considered such an analogy merely unfortunate, had he not abrogated the human capacity for suffering from a retarded person in a second comparison to animals (p. 323). In describing a retarded woman chained by the neck to a dog's running-wire in the yard, he denied that she was suffering because "she was a mere animal, well cared-for as an animal." Nosworthy (1907) probably expressed latent sentiments most honestly when, in all seriousness, she raised the question whether the feeble-minded constitute a separate species, and then designed a study to investigate this matter.

Humans can be dehumanized even below the animal and vegetative level, as when they are called "waste products" (Barr, 1902, p. 165; Anderson, 1918, p. 537) or "by-products" (Mac-

Murchy, as quoted in Murdoch, 1909, p. 66; Southard, 1915, p. 316). Southard continued to ask: "... it becomes a question with us, what to do with these waste materials."

Concern With Prevention

It should be obvious from reading the indictment that retardation was considered to be hereditary. Some quotations follow: "We have only begun to understand the importance of feeble-mindedness. In Massachusetts there are families who have been paupers for many generations. Some of the members were born or even conceived in the poorhouse" (Fernald, 1912, p. 91). "No feeble-minded mother will ever have a child absolutely normal in every respect" (Johnson, 1908, p. 333). "Feeble-mindedness is hereditary and transmitted as surely as any other character" (Goddard, 1912, p. 117). "... In two-thirds of the cases feeble-mindedness is caused by feeble-mindedness..." (Goddard, 1915, p. 308). "It is possible that a real eugenic survey of a given locality might show that 90% of the feeble-mindedness in that locality was contributed by 5% of the families in that community" (Fernald, 1915, p. 294). "Degeneracy, once permitted to invade a lineage, can never be *wholly* eradicated; lessened materially, and even reduced to a minimum it may be, but sooner or later, in one generation or another, a defective is bound to appear." "... There are at least 328,000 mental and moral defectives at large, perpetrating, unrestrained, the defilement of the race." "... Imbecility will breed imbecility and where there is a trace of feeble-mindedness in a family it is sure, sooner or later, to reappear, the defective 'germ plasma' producing an abnormal" (Barr, 1915, pp. 361-363). "We must come to recognize feeble-mindedness, idiocy, imbecility, and insanity as largely communicable conditions or diseases, just as the ordinary physician recognizes smallpox, diptheria, etc., as communicable" (Sprattling, 1901, p. 409). When Goddard (1912, pp. 283-284) was asked whether feeble-mindedness could not be the result of poverty and malnutrition, he said: "There is not the slightest evidence that malnutrition, or any environmental condition can produce feeble-mindedness" (Goddard, 1912, pp. 283-284).

A logical conclusion of the foregoing line of reasoning was that aside from euthanasia, only prevention of reproduction of the retarded could reduce their number: "At least, let us wipe out the stain of legalizing the production of idiocy, imbecility, insanity, and crime" (Knight, 1898, p. 308). "This national body of charity workers, together with its associate bodies, has done a mighty work in the past score of years in helping to project the establishment of these institutions; but its helping hand must ever be extended, and its heart and soul be strong in purpose, until legislation shall put in force necessary preventive measures that will stop the increase and wipe out the degeneracy of the past, until humanity shall recognize the need of pure living and right purpose" (Polglase, 1901, p. 190).

"The one effective way to diminish the number of the feeble-minded in future generations is to prevent the birth of those who would transmit feeble-mindedness to their descendants." "Indeed, the results of eugenic research are so impressive that we are almost convinced that we are in possession of knowledge which would enable us to markedly diminish the number of the feeble-minded in a few generations if segregation or surgical sterilization of all known defectives were possible" (Fernald, 1915, p. 290).

Barr, in 1915 (p. 361) wrote an article entitled "The Prevention of Mental Defect, The Duty of the Hour," which began: "That the prevention of the transmission of mental defect is the paramount duty of the hour, is a truism not to be questioned." The article contained the following memorable lines: "... One cannot fail to recognize the necessity for the enforcement of measures which experience has demonstrated as absolutely needful steps toward prevention, viz: The separation, sequestration and asexualization of degenerates..." (1915, p. 364).

Other writers added: "The successful control of amentia is the most imperative of public duties." "... Conserve the mental virility and moral integrity of the race" (Schlapp, 1915, pp. 328; 321). "The present generation is the trustee for the inherent quality as well as for the material welfare of the future generations" (Fernald, 1915, p. 295). "... We absolutely cannot afford to wait" (G. H. Knight, 1898, p. 307).

Much study was given to the means of prevention. Private and public study and action groups proliferated. In 1903, there existed a "Committee on Colonies For and Segregation of Defectives" of the National Conference on Charities and Correction. By 1915, seven states had public commissions (Schlapp, 1915) much like our governors' committees today. Several other states had unofficial commissions, and several cities had commissions much like today's mayors' committees. In Philadelphia in 1916, there was headquartered a national organization, entitled "The Committee on Provision for the Feeble-minded," that had as its purpose "to disseminate knowledge concerning the extent and menace of feeble-mindedness and to suggest and initiate methods for its control and ultimate eradication from the American people" (as quoted by Johnstone, 1916, pp. 206-207). This committee was credited with being instrumental in giving 1,100 lectures to about 250,000 people; in establishing institutions in nine states that had none; in increasing the number of existing institutions in five states; and in extending the sizes of existing institutions in four states (Davies, 1930).

One of the more influential study groups was the Eugenics Section of The American (Cattle) Breeders Association, which, curiously, later became the American Eugenics Society and the sponsor of the respected contemporary Journal *Eugenics Quarterly*. This group issued a well-known report (summarized by Van Wagenen, 1914) that considered 10 possible measures, judging only two to be practical: sterilization, and segregation of those retarded persons capable of reproduction. In general, there was a "... keen interest in everything pertaining to the mentally deficient both in Europe and in this country. The realization of the vast extent of mental defect, the inexorable requirements of the modern graded school systems with the study of the resulting retardation, the popular application of the Binet and other psychological tests, are some of the causes of this interest. Mental deficiency has become a subject of vital and pressing significance to physicians, psychologists, teachers, court officials, social workers, and legislators. The subject is being studied from medical, biological, pedagogical, psychological, sociological, economic, and eugenic points of view. The field of mental defect has been so broadened and extended as to include all the professional disciplines" (1913, cited by De Prospo, 1966, p. 38).

Belief in the genetic causation of retardation had some convenient aspects. By proposing that most social problems would be solved if the poorer members of society would stop having children, one could feel freed from a sense of responsibility for bad social condition. Furthermore, one was relieved from the worry of the effects of slum conditions upon children, if one could believe that many such children were genetically inferior to begin with. It is probably no coincidence that the indictment period overlapped with periods during which Social Darwinism and laissez-faire socio-economic policies were prominent.

Failure of Preventive Marriage Laws

In order to understand how institutions for the retarded in the United States developed as they did, we must understand the failure of alternative provisions.

During the indictment period, the only hope seen was in the prevention of procreation of individuals likely to produce retarded persons. Three methods suggested themselves: forbidding the mating of retarded persons by law; preventing procreation, of those retarded persons who might mate, by sterilization; and preventing both mating and procreation, by means of segregation.

Outlawing of procreation was attempted early in the alarmist period. In about 1895, House Bill 681, containing the following provision, was passed in Connecticut:

"Every man who shall carnally know any female under the age of forty-five years who is epileptic, imbecile, feeble-minded, or a pauper, shall be imprisoned in the State prison not less than three years. Every man who is epileptic who shall carnally know any female under the age of forty-five years, and every female under the age of forty-five years who shall consent to be carnally known by any man who is epileptic, imbecile, or feeble-minded, shall be imprisoned in the State prison not less than three years" (Beedy, 1895, p. 468). Similar bills were soon passed, and some of these bills are still on the books today (1968). A national marriage law to prohibit marriage to the feeble-minded and insane was proposed as early as 1897 by Wells (1897), and was widely supported. In 1899, what is now the American Association on Mental Deficiency appointed a committee to explore cooperation with the National Conference on Charities and Correction, the Prison Congress, the Medico-Psychological Society, and other bodies that might be interested in supporting restrictive marriage laws (*J. Psycho-Asthenics*, 1899, 3, pp. 194-195). By 1900, Wilmarth (1902, p. 156) had this to say: "There are only two remedies for the abatement of this evil in the class of which we speak today. The seclusion of feeble-minded and epileptic adults, especially females between the ages of fifteen and forty-five who are liable to become willing subjects to man's rascality, and the passing of such laws as shall prevent the marriage of defectives, or the living together as man and wife of any one with a defective person."

The ineffectiveness of marriage laws was soon recognized: "Restrictive marriage laws are no doubt advisable, but . . . unavailing because the unfit reproduce their kind regardless of marriage laws" (Murdoch, 1913, pp. 36-37). Alas, sex, even less than alcohol later on, was not easily outlawed. However, sterilization suggested itself as a reasonable alternative.

Failure of Preventive Sterilization

Sterilization, or as it was also called, asexualization, and unsexing, was apparently first advocated to a significant degree in the mid-1890's. Like virtually all administrative measures which nondeviant people design to manage deviant ones, sterilization was often rationalized as being to the retarded person's advantage. Barr (1902) called for ". . . invoking the aid of surgical interference to secure . . . greater liberty, therefore, greater happiness to the individual" (p. 5).

In 1902, Nicholson (p. 495) ended the discussion of papers on the "feeble-minded and epileptic" at the Detroit National Conference on Charities and Correction by stating that "the only way to get rid of such imbeciles is to stop raising them." A more direct tack was taken by Perry (1903, p. 254): ". . . It would now be well to prepare our several states to call to our assistance the surgeon's knife to prevent the entailing of this curse upon innocent numbers of yet unborn children." Barr asked: " . . . Knowing the certain transmission of such taint, how can one fail to appreciate the advantage of prevention over penalty, or to recognize as the most beneficent instrument of law the surgeon's knife preventing increase. And why not? We guard against all epidemics, are quick to quarantine small-pox, and we exclude the Chinese; but we take no steps to eliminate this evil from the body social" (1902, p. 163).

It was soon recognized that sterilization, in order to reduce the number of the retarded to an appreciable extent, had to be compulsory, and such laws were passed throughout the nation and generally upheld by the courts.[6] However, it was also found that sterilization laws were only slightly more enforceable than mating laws; that not all the retarded were reached by the laws; and that sterilization would not prevent as many cases of retardation as had been thought: "Compulsory surgical sterilization of all defectives is proposed as a radical method for preventing the hereditary transmission of feeble-mindedness. At least six states have passed laws authorizing or requiring this operation. In no state, however, has this remedy been applied on a large scale. There are many objections to this plan. The friends of the patients are not willing to have the operation performed. The normal 'carriers' of defect would not be affected. The presence of these sterile people in the community, with unimpaired sexual desire and capacity would be direct encouragement of vice and a prolific source of venereal disease. Sterilization would not be a safe and effective substitute for permanent segregation and control" (Fernald, 1912, pp. 95-96).

"Sterilization of the feeble-minded is logically the solution for the problem of prevention of propagation of the mentally unfit where feeble-mindedness is due to heredity. Practically, despite legislation, it has never worked because it is purely an intellectual remedy. It has never considered the prolonged period of preparation and education necessary to change deep-seated primitive attitudes. There may come a time when sterilization of the unfit will be worked into our program, but it will be only when the general level of enlightenment on social problems is materially raised by slow growth" (Taft, 1918, p. 545). "The sterilization of feeble-minded is now universally acknowledged to be impracticable, principally because the hereditary influence in this field has not been quantitatively determined, because the operation is dangerous, the idea more or less revolting and, possibly, because it is not in consonance with the religious thought of a certain portion of the community. Sterilization, therefore, need not be further discussed at this time" (Cornell, 1915, p. 338).

Failure of Preventive Segregation

Once mating laws, sterilization, and other measures had been recognized as ineffective or unacceptable in preventing the spread of the retardation menace, only segregation (Fernald in 1915 called it "strict sexual quarantine") remained, and it was advanced with utmost vigor by the workers in the field. First, of course, it had to be rationalized to be, at least in part, for the welfare of the retarded. An editorial in the *Journal of Psycho-Asthenics* in 1899 asked: "Of what is a high-grade imbecile deprived on entering a well-conducted institution?", and concluded he would only be deprived of deprivation. Winspear (1895, p. 163) reasoned as follows: "A moment's thought, and the fact is plain that unprotected feeble-minded women of full physical development are in constant danger themselves, and are always a menace to society, — a twofold reason why custodial care for this class should be the paramount idea in the State's provision for the feeble-minded. Thus their proper care and protection is a twice blessed charity, in that it blesses the recipient of the State's bounties and blesses society by the removing of a great evil therefrom."

More direct arguments included the following: "Shall we turn these irresponsibles loose to undo the work of the past and redouble that of the future? Surely history would not write our names among the wise" (Barr, 1899, p. 211). "... I think we need to write it very large, in characters that he who runs may read, to convince the world that by permanent separation only is the imbecile to be safe-guarded from certain deterioration and society from depredation, contamination and increase of a pernicious element" (Barr, 1902, p. 6). "But all of them whether able of productive labor or wholly helpless, or of any grade between these extremes, ought to be permanent wards of the state so long as they shall live" (Johnson, 1901, p. 411).

In 1905, ratarded adult males were characterized in the Maine Senate as "town loafers and incapables," "petty thieves," "incendiaries," sources of "unspeakable debauchery" which "pollute the whole life of young boys" and who "have illegitimate children every one of whom is predestined to be defective mentally, criminal or an outcast of some sort." Such individuals were to be placed in an institution, and the institution, in turn, was to be placed in an isolated spot.

When sterilization failed to halt the "spread of retardation", society turned to a last resort— "strict sexual quarantine." Separate facilities were built across the country solely to protect society from "feebleminded women of child-bearing age." (1927)

These measures were to save the communities of the state of Maine from "terrible menace" and "economic burdens" of the feeble-minded whose "uncontrolled life and movements threatened great harm to society" (quoted by Levinson, 1960).

"The only just and humane and civilized way of stopping the transmission of defectiveness is by segregation" (Johnson, 1908, pp. 333-334). "Every effort must be made to get these defectives out of society . . . " " . . . the degeneracy must cease *here*" (Johnstone, 1904, pp. 66, 65).

Consistent with the proposal advanced earlier that retardation should be treated as a communicable disease, Murdoch (1909) gave a paper entitled "Quarantine Mental Defectives." Johnstone (1905, p. 66) called for a " . . . quarantine of this social disease . . . "

"On the most important proposition of all—who gets born—last year Governor Foss vetoed an increased appropriation for our second school for the feeble-minded. This year, however, provision was made for two new cottages, which will hold two hundred inmates, and cut off by, perhaps, half that number of source of supply of the unhappy and unfit among future generations. The righteous have sworn the segregation of all the feeble-minded for 1925" (Reports from States, 1912, p. 525).

Not only were the retarded to be segregated from society, but even within institutions, men and women were strictly segregated, almost to a paranoid and bizarre degree: "The institution that places . . . boys and girls anywhere near each other . . . will never do its part in the work of preventing feeble-mindedness in the community." "The institution superintendent who allows feeble-minded boys and feeble-minded girls to work together even in the garden, is running the risk of a second generation of illegitimate feeble-minded children" (Cornell, 1915, pp. 33-34).

If it was difficult to keep men and women apart within an institution, then separate institutions for the sexes might be the answer, and a number of such institutions were maintained or built: "Custodial care for feeble-minded women of full physical development, in distinctly separate institutions, which was at first considered by many a doubtful experiment, has proved a grand success, and should be followed by every other state in this country" (Winspear, 1895, p. 161).

The extreme in segregation was advocated by Barr who proposed the establishment of one or more national institutions or reservations (Barr, 1897; 1899; 1902; Dunlap, 1899) similar to the management of another large deviant group in America, *viz.*, the Indians: "The National government has provided for the Mute, the Negro, and the Indian—then, why not for this branch of population increasing as rapidly as they, and becoming yearly more inimical to national prosperity. A reservation set apart, affording facilities for agricultural pursuits as well as all the varied industries of a town, would provide an outlet for the surplus population of our institutions, to find there a home with definite life aims constantly realized. Such a colony, under such restrictions and protective care as our experience has proven is essential, a congregate number of institutions, so to speak . . . " (Barr, 1897, p. 13). "Protected from the world and the world from them, these children of the nation, instead of as now, its standing peril, would be a constant object lesson, at once a reproof and a warning to guide us to that 'statlier Eden of simpler manners, purer laws' which the twentieth century shall usher in" (Barr, 1899, p. 212).

Workers in the field were, at times, rather unrealistic. They exhorted the public to marry on a eugenic rather than emotional basis, and to forego marriage altogether if presumably inheritable detrimental traits were observed in their families. Similarly, some workers appealed to parents to institutionalize their children voluntarily: "Greater efforts must be made to have the great public know of the defectives, so that we shall not be accused of having axes to grind when we ask for more provision for them. Institution men must encourage visits, give out information and indeed, conduct a campaign of education, so that in the first place the unwillingness of parents to send their children shall be changed to eagerness, and then will follow the demands of public opinion and the concessions of legislatures" (Johnstone, 1906, p. 237).

At the end of the founding period, legislatures had been asked to *permit* residents to stay. As late as 1902 (Wilmarth, 1902), discharges from institutions were easy and informal. However, the tone changed during the alarmist period, and increasingly, laws and rules *mandated* legal and quasi-permanent commitments rather than voluntary and temporary ones: "... parents brought their children after a commitment by a local magistrate and in many cases subsequently tormented the superintendent of the institution by demands for their release. The superintendent was so harassed that he, himself, made a rule that he would receive no children unless they were committed to him by the courts, so that the state was made a legal guardian of the children in the institution. We are happy to say that this principle was afterwards embodied in an act of the legislature, in effect October, 1914, which provided that all admissions and discharges from the state institution at Spring City should be by court commitment" (Cornell, 1915, p. 332).

Since segregation was for the protection of society, it was only logical that commitments should be compulsory: "Segregation does not mean the opening of a boarding home by the state in which parents may place their feeble-minded children, have them trained by much labor, to the point where they become dangerous to the community if allowed at liberty, and then remove them and turn them loose" (Cornell, 1915, pp. 331-332). Johnstone (1908a) recommended that admission of "degenerates" require a trial and an indeterminate sentence. Release would also be only by trial, although little need for such trials was seen: "The only possible reason we can urge for their being set free is a sentimental one" (p. 114).

Apparently, Illinois was the first state to require court commitments, as of 1915 (Harley, 1917), to the exclusion of all other types of admission. Laws of this nature were criticized, not on legalistic or humanistic grounds, but because they might discourage parents from admitting their children (e.g., Carson, 1906).

One is left with the distinct impression that sensing the impending failure to segregate all the retarded, workers in the field vented their frustration by striving to increase the degree of segregation of the retarded who were already in their custody. Also, the fact that retarded residents had been released into the community both before and after the indictment period would appear to indicate that the decline of successful rehabilitations early during the indictment was an artifact of institutional policy. In other words, residents were not released by the institution personnel because the personnel did not believe that residents could or should succeed. For instance, until 1967, retarded persons in Nebraska gained entrance to the state institution only by court commitment; once committed, they could, until 1963, only be released if they were sterilized or otherwise incapable of reproduction. To this day (1968), the law requires that release be preceded by a time-consuming expensive review by a sterilization board.

Our historical review now approaches another critical point. We must consider that the professionals in the field were thoroughly convinced that the survival of society required that the largest number of retarded persons be institutionalized as fast as possible. "Assuredly, if we are to rise to the responsibility of the times, to grapple with this enemy one hundred thousand strong, which enters all homes alike and threatens the very life-blood of the nation, we must enlarge our borders and extend our operations. We need space, and yet more space, and who than we better fitted to claim it?" (Barr, 1897, pp. 12-13). Here, however, the professionals encountered limitations in funding of institutions, and the public and legislatures were not channeling additional funds as fast as the professionals thought they should. "The public, while liberal in all its charities, demands that the funds so appropriated should be wisely and economically expended, and that the cost should be kept as low as possible, consistent with the best methods of carrying on the work" (Wilmarth, 1902, p. 152). "Our taxpayers are already groaning under the burden of caring for the actual imbecile and the epileptic" (Fernald, 1908, p. 116).

First, there was an attempt to convince the public that financial support of institutions would save money in the long run: "This special care is now recognized as not only charitable, but economical and conservative. Each hundred dollars invested now saves a thousand in the next generation" (Fernald, 1893, p. 221).

"As a simple business proposition no state can make a better investment, or one actually paying larger dividends, than to insure that the feeble-minded women of child-bearing age are prevented from bringing defective paupers into the world to go on reproducing themselves in geometrical ratio. The direct money saving from this result alone in a few generations would represent a sum equal to the cost of maintenance of the entire feeble-minded population of the state. The much quoted history of the Jukes family showed that in sveenty-five years the community paid over one and one-quarter millions of dollars for caring for the paupers and prosecuting the criminals who were the direct descendants of two feeble-minded sisters" (Fernald, 1904, pp. 384-385).

"If my estimate is within bounds, the entire money cost of removing this dreadful stain from our nation would be, after an expenditure by each state of an average amount of less than half a million for lands and building, a maintenance fund of about ten cents per annum for each of the inhabitants of the United States.

"How foolish is the action of the public in saving such a small amount at the spigot and wasting so profusely at the bung! Ought not this question be made a burning one? Ought not every one convinced of these facts to cry aloud, and spare not, until the legislature of every state shall have the facts burned into their hearts and consciences, as they are now into ours?

"Unfortunately, it is the superintendents of state institutions who are usually compelled to propose the extension of their work. And then they are accused of extravagance, of a desire to glorify themselves at the expense of the taxpayer. The truth is that they are the ones who feel most keenly the needs that they assert; and, if they do not speak, all will be silent" (Johnson, 1896, p. 218). "The cost of segregation will be large, but not so large as the present cost of caring for these same persons, to say nothing of their progeny in future generations" (Fernald, 1915, p. 295).

But some years earlier, in one of the first public statements of indictment, Walk (1890, p. 441) had predicted correctly: "If you are going to shut up all the idiotic and feebleminded where they can do no harm, you must do it in a cheap way." "If it cannot be done at a cheap rate, you can never get money to do it."

The professionals were caught between their convictions about the absolute necessity to segregate the largest numbers of the retarded, and the limitations of legislative appropriations. In desperation, they developed three interrelated plans: (1) by reducing per capita costs, more people could be admitted on a given budget; (2) by increasing the population of institutions, per capita costs would come down; (3) by having higher-functioning residents work the land and take care of lower-functioning residents. If these proposals were implemented, perhaps costs could be so reduced that eventually all the retarded might be enfolded in the institution. This thinking intensified the trend toward economy discussed earlier as a concomitant of the pity period.

"It is true that the cost of these schools has been great in the past, and when we consider the number to be provided for—at least ten times as many as are now in the institutions—the total cost would appear prohibitory of this plan. But just as soon as it is demonstrated that a large proportion is self-supporting; that the improvables can be cared for, with decency and humanity, at a very moderate ratio of expense, by utilizing the labor of the trained higher grades; that only the younger ones, who belong to the educable grade, and a few of the lowest grade violent and dangerous idiots, require a high per capita cost—it seems probable that the means to gather in and care for the whole class will be forthcoming. When that period arrives, the number of idiots and imbeciles in the nation will cease to increase, and, if other classes of degenerates can also be brought under control, the number may diminish very rapidly" (Johnson, 1898, p. 471).

An argument that became very popular was that since most community breadwinners must support three or more persons, a retarded resident who was one-third as productive as a community worker would be self-supporting. "When the feeble-minded are recognized in childhood and trained properly, many of them are capable of being supported at low cost under institution supervision" (Fernald, 1915, p. 295). At least for a while, apparently everyone believed that self-sufficiency and complete segregation of the retarded was to be found in the work potential of the residents. "The only hope that I can see of the state taking complete care and responsibility of all idiots and imbeciles is that all those who have been trained, those of the higher grade who are susceptible to training, who have been trained to the highest degree possible for them, shall be so usefully employed that they may be practically self-supporting. We need a great deal of low grade labor, and a great deal of labor can be performed by laborers of a low degree of intelligence. In the care of the lowest custodial grade of imbeciles, in the care of epileptics of low grade, there is a great deal of labor available among our trained imbeciles; and they can do no better work than to exercise such care in an institution" (Johnson, 1902, p. 492).

Beginning in about 1880, so-called farm colonies had come into vogue. In essence, they were institutions that specialized in making the less retarded residents as self-supporting as possible by having them farm large tracts of land. Knight (1891), Fernald (1902), Mastin (1916a, 1916b), and Bernstein (1918, 1920) presented key models of such facilities. The belief developed that with enough land, an institution could actually become self-supporting. The rule of thumb that appeared to materialize out of nowhere (e.g., Osborne, 1891) was: one acre per resident. "Having decided upon the number of inmates, at least one acre of land for each inmate should be purchased" (Fish, 1892, p. 163). "It has been conceded for years that each institution should be provided with at least one acre per inmate; and, as we grow in years, it is thought by some that even more than this is needed" (Powell, 1897, p. 295). "The colony estate should be large, fully an acre to each individual. It is far better to have a little too much land than too little. We have at Sonyea 1895 acres, on which it is proposed ultimately to place 1800 people" (Sprattling, 1903, p. 261). "The site for an institution should comprise 1 acre of land for every pupil when the institution has reached its maximum" (Wallace, 1924, p. 258).

With such a rule of thumb, institutions soon became monstrous in extent: "The colony farm for the adult feeble-minded of Massachusetts is one of the largest of its kind in the world, covering several square miles of land" (Johnson, 1903, p. 250). "The Craig Colony estate (in New York), three miles long and a mile and half wide, . . ." (Sprattling, 1903, p. 261). Powell (1897) provided detailed information on U.S. institutions, including number of residents and land holdings. If one computes the average acreage per resident, one arrives at a figure of 1.01. By 1915, Bureau of Census (1919) data indicate that average per resident acreage had risen to 2.47 or 2.99, depending on how the average is computed. By 1922, the heyday (hay-day?) of farm colonies seemed to be past, as average acreage was down to 1.31, and by 1933, it had fallen further to .62 (Bureau of the Census, 1926, 1935).

Doren had been superintendent in Ohio for many years, and in 1884, he reported that 24-30 percent of his residents "become capable of self-support" (Kerlin, 1884, p. 251). In the mid-1880's, Doren made a fateful boast: "The superintendent of the Ohio institution has made a proposition to the legislature of that state like this: Give me the land and allow me to gather the idiotic and imbecile population now under public care together, and I agree that the institution shall be made self-sustaining, and I will pay back to the state the price of the land" (Byers, 1890, p. 441). As widely quoted and repeated, (e.g., Kerlin, 1886; Knight, 1891, 1892; Fernald, 1893; Follet, 1895; Bicknell, 1896; Byers, 1916), Doren was said to have stated that 1,000 acres would suffice to carry out his claim.

"I am quite sure that with sufficient farm land, and in connection with our present institution, the adult able-bodied imbeciles of both sexes could be kept in our state at a weekly cost of not more than $1 per capita in addition to what the farm would produce" (Johnson, 1896, p. 218). By 1902, Johnson (p. 492) stated that the average annual maintenance cost in an Indiana farm colony was actually down to $32, which must have referred to a very select sub-group, as overall maintenance costs in Indiana were about $136 in 1902.

Residents were worked to the limit of their capacity, and, it appears, sometimes even beyond: "They should be under such conditions that many of them shall not cost the tax-payer anything ... the state must ... say to them 'We will take care of you: you shall be happy and well cared for and clean and useful; but you shall labor and earn your bread in the sweat of your face according to the divine command.' That is what ought to be done with the whole class of degenerates, just so far as it is possible to do it" (Johnson, 1901, p. 411). Mastin (1916b, pp. 34-35) declared that what was "... heart-breaking and unprofitable work for normal persons ... " would be " ... 'particularly fitted' ... " and " ... agreeable, if not joyful occupation ... " for the retarded. " ... You cannot work those boys too hard. If they work them as hard as they can they will not practice the vices ... " "Let them go out and work just as hard as they will work. That is what they have to do for me when they work on the farm. They work so that when they come in at night they go to bed and sleep. Then they get up the next morning and go to work again, and I am very sure that the farmers who are working them the hardest are keeping them the best in line of good behavior. Miss Boehne suggests that the boy was overworked. Of course, we know that there are some tubercular conditions among the feeble-minded, that should be considered. About half of our population are subject to these same conditions" (Bernstein, in Fernald, 1912, p. 105).[7]

Residents might not only be worked like animals, it seemed, but also received about as much (or even less) medical care: Mastin (1916a, 1916b) and Swan (1908) boasted that medical expenses for over a year in one of the Massachusetts farm colonies was a total of less than one dollar for all 50 resident males combined. This stands quite in contrast to Fernald's earlier (1902, p. 489) description of a farm colony, prior to the cost squeeze: "They have their baseball nines and their football teams. They go coasting and skating in the winter and swimming in the brook in the summer. *What more can a boy want?*" (Fernald, 1902, p. 489).

There was much self-delusion and falsification of facts regarding maintenance costs, and I found it difficult to distinguish between claims as to: how many residents were discharged as self-supporting; how many were considered potentially self-supporting in the community; what the maintenance costs were, and what the maintenance costs might have been. "Dr. Walter E. Fernald, of Massachusetts, in speaking on this subject, says: 'Not over 10 or 15 percent of our inmates can be made self-supporting, in the sense of going out into the community and securing and retaining a situation, and prudently spending their earnings. With all our training we cannot give our pupils that indispensable something known as good, plain common sense.'" (Carson, 1898, p. 295). The superintendent of Lapeer, Michigan, claimed: "Twenty-five per cent. of our inmates would be self-supporting if the work were put into their hands to do" (Polglase, 1900, p. 425). "Mr. Alexander Johnson says that in his institution 50 per cent. of his inmates are self-supporting" (Fox, 1900, p. 431).

"The proportion of the feeble-minded who may be made to earn their own living, under control, is variously estimated. The superintendents of at least two of the large training schools, both men of practical common sense, place the estimate as high as 50 percent. of the whole number admitted. It is instructive to notice that estimates of this kind tend to become larger, especially as made by the managers of institutions which have a large acreage of farming and fruit-growing lands" (Johnson, 1898, p. 469).

"The cost of maintenance for mixed classes of patients in colonies after the population reaches 600 to 700 will be less than for the insane; while colonies for selected cases only should not require more than $75.00 to $80.00 a patient a year, and under ideal conditions even less" (Sprattling, 1903, p. 267).

"Build them up as high as you can, keep them where they are safe and will be industrious and half of them, perhaps more than that, may be entirely self-supporting and no burden upon the tax-payer at all" (Johnson, 1905, p. 537). While records show that maintenance costs in Pennsylvania were about $175 a year, superintendent Kerlin was quoted as follows: "Dr. Kerlin tells me that, when they had three hundred inmates, it cost them twenty thousand dollars for expenses. Now with seven hundred inmates, it does not cost any more. What does that mean? It means that the feeble-minded themselves are doing the work and helping to solve their own problems" (Barrows, 1888, p. 400). Even though Kerlin was probably misquoted, it is of significance that prominent workers in the field were ready to believe that costs were down to $29 per year. Fernald can be seen to be stretching the truth a bit in the following statement: "The average running expenses of these institutions have been gradually and largely reduced by this utilization of the industrial abilities of the trained inmates. At the Pennsylvania institutions the per capita cost of all the inmates has been reduced from $300 to a little over $100 per annum..." (1893, p. 218). The records showed Pennsylvania costs to vary from 152 to 175 between 1889 and 1894. Johnson (1900) and Bernstein (1918b) gave boastful papers on "self-sustaining" residents even as the maintenance costs at Bernstein's Institution (Rome, N.Y.) were $150 a year. A breakdown of the 1928 average maintenance costs of 24 farm colonies for males at Rome State School showed a range of $186-508, with a mean of $260 and a median of $232 (Davies, 1930, p. 225).

While residents' work, and development of farm colonies, did not make the institutions self-sufficient, costs were, indeed, reduced, held constant, or held down to an astonishing degree. "Many years of experience have taught us economy of administration; and, while the efficiency of service is constantly increased, the cost of maintenance is gradually diminished. It will be found, after making due allowance for the number cared for and the difference in cost of supplies at various points, that the average per capita cost is remarkably uniform" (Wilmarth, 1902, p. 153).

Superintendents vied with each other in reducing cost, and aside from farming, another way to economize was to develop institutional architecture that was "plain but substantial": "The buildings themselves should be exceedingly plain and simple. What intrinsic reason is there for building more expensive structures than middleclass people build for their own dwellings in the same community?" (Fernald, 1902, p. 490). "Plain, substantial buildings, with modern sanitary toilet facilities, and of architectural beauty, but no filigrees, are what we need" (Johnstone, 1907, p. 323). "... Permanence in construction with low maintenance cost..." (Kirkbride, 1916, p. 255). "The institution that we provide for the feeble-minded should be constructed and maintained at a moderate cost. There has been a disposition to build marble palaces for the most degenerate members of the community..." (Cornell, 1915, p. 334).

In 1893, Fernald (p. 220) stated that capital expenditures per bed should be no more than $400. By 1916, Byers (p. 227) asserted flatly: "The state that expends more than $300.00 per bed for the buildings and equipment of a colony from one to three hundred inmates, spends too much."

Stripping the residents' environment of amenities and comforts so as to cut costs was accompanied by tortuous rationalizations: "As a rule, mental defectives are descended from the poorer classes, and for generations their people have lived in homes having few conveniences. To expect them to be content in a great city institution with its up-to-date furnishings and equipment, and its strict routine, is unreasonable. They find little comfort in steam heat and polished floors; and the glare of electric lights too often adds to their restlessness. It is useless to hope that they will ever be happy as it is possible for them to be if we do not gratify their love for open spaces or provide for them the opportunity to live the simple out-of-door life under circumstances which will enable them not only to keep busy but to enjoy the fruits of their labor" (Mastin, 1916a, p. 245). A statement uncomfortably close to suggesting human warehousing was attributed to Fernald by Kirkbride (1916, p. 253): "It is obvious that if large numbers of the feeble-minded are to be cared for the cost of housing them must be reduced to a point where it cannot be criticized by the business man and the tax-payer." "The ornamental or decorative features of the old-time institution will have to go, if this is to be accomplished." "We have only begun to utilize the beautiful, well-proportioned commercial type of buildings, such as the General Electric Co., the Bridgeport Arms Co., etc. are building."

In the early days, costs at Elwyn in Pennsylvania had been $350; by about 1890, they were down to about $175 (Kerlin, 1890), and to $152 in 1893 (see Appendix 1). Wilbur estimated that average maintenance costs were about $200 in 1888 (p. 108). Powell (1897, p. 296) thought that cost could be reduced to about $150 or even $125. Almost in desperation, Cornell (1915, p. 334) exclaimed: "Until we get the per capita cost of the high grade feeble-minded down less than $100 per year there will be objection to their segregation on the ground of expense."

Although attempts to become self-supporting failed, the relative true expenditures hit a low during the indictment period, not to be equalled even during the depth of the depression (see Appendix 1). As costs went down (at least in relation to the value of the dollar), admissions went up. Successively larger institutions were rationalized as being of ideal size, and as size grew, the rationalizers moved on from one rationale to the next. "One thousand inmates should, in my opinion, be the maximum number under one management" (Fish, 1892, p. 163). Knowing what was to come, we shudder as a small voice of caution is brushed aside: "Mr. Garret has referred to the fact that, in the establishment of an institution for a thousand of the feeble-minded, the identity of the individual child may be lost sight of. I think there is possibly some ground for that fear; but in our institution, which is planned to care for a thousand eventually, we do not find any lack of the same personal care and interest on the part of caretakers and attendants. Their enthusiasm and interest are just as great as in the beginning of the work. I do not anticipate any evil results in extension of the work on the line suggested" (Fish, 1892, p. 349).

H. M. Greene (1884) and Wilmarth (1900) suggested that institutions not exceed 1,000. Murdoch (1909) expressed the hope that his institution would remain at 1,340, but by 1913 he had capitulated, calling for 2,000-3,000. R. A. Greene (1927) called an institution for 1,000-1,500 "ideal." Sprattling (1903, p. 261) was planning an institution for 1,800. Hart (1896, p. 488) of Minnesota said: "Our buildings are excellent; but they sadly need enlargement. We could have, I think, 2,000. The demand is convincing and unanswerable." "I do not believe that the size of an institution should be so limited. It seems to me that two or three thousand can be cared for in one institution when the possibilities of grading and grouping are so great. Why should we not have towns of them? If the superintendent is an organizer, it is a benefit to the state to take care of three thousand in one institution. I would not put any limit to the number that a man can properly handle" (Smith, 1913, pp. 39-40). Finally, the cork was pulled altogether: Polk (Pennsylvania), which had been built to relieve crowding at Elwyn, and which had had 1,200 residents in 1906 (Murdoch, 1906), had grown to 2,300 residents, 84 percent overcrowding, and a waiting list of 500 by 1928 (Watkins, 1928); Columbus (Ohio) had 2,430, with construction under-

The original pencil notation found on the back of this photograph reads: "Girls working in canning plant." Such institutional peonage was euphemistically called "training." (1927)

After the summer fruit was canned, it was moved to storage areas on the institutional grounds. The intentions of these work efforts were clearly to make the institutions, not the resident, self-sufficient. (1927)

way for 240 more, and funds appropriated for yet another 700. Superintendent Emerich threw up his hands; much like Fernald (1893), he said, in his presidential address to what is now the American Association on Mental Deficiency: "It seems easier to get the legislature to appropriate funds for more buildings, for the institutions we already have, than it does to get new institutions, but as the institution at Columbus is now so large that the Superintendent cannot keep in touch with the inmates, it might just as well have a population of 10,000 as 3,000" (Emerich, 1917b, p. 74; see also Emerich, 1917a).

A peculiar but commonly repeated twist of logic in support of enlargement was advanced as early as 1895: "Each year the number committed to our care has been a considerable increase over that of the preceding; and we have now reached a population at which our extended accommodations are exhausted, with numerous applicants knocking at our doors for admission. Provisions to meet this demand are already near completion. This numerical statement is a most gratifying proof of the good work of the institution, and positive evidence of the full confidence of all public-minded, charitable citizens" (Winspear, 1895, p. 163).[8]

The menace image of the retarded, and the perceived necessity to farm large tracts of land for large groups of residents, combined to result in the locating or relocating of most institutions away from population centers and in rural areas where farm land could be had inexpensively. This exacerbated the trend toward isolation begun during the pity period: "Massachusetts has purchased for its school for feeble-minded at Waverly, 2,000 acres of cheap land, sixty-one miles from the parent institution and has already established on it three colony groups of about 50 boys each, the two extreme groups separated by two miles. These boys live amidst simple, plain environments and in almost primitive, yet comfortable style. Dr. Fernald is there making a practical demonstration of the possibility of carrying out the plan above indicated, in a manner both economical to the state and conducive to the best interests and happiness of the boys themselves. The plan is economical because of the simplicity of the equipment required. There is no necessity here for expensive buildings, like schools or hospitals, with their necessary apparatus" (Rogers, 1903, p. 257).

In 1913, J. M. Murdock (p. 36) called for institutions of 2,000-3,000 located ". . . far from any large city and rather isolated . . . " and on 3,000-4,000 acres of land. By 1930, isolation had become so accepted and real that he reversed himself slightly, advocating, in all seriousness, that institutions " . . . should not be too isolated, and should be near enough to a village where employees may do their shopping, find social interest, and entertainment" (p. 243).

For a long time, Johnstone (brother-in-law of A. Johnson) and Kirkbride were the only ones to raise a voice in partial opposition to the prevailing thinking. For several years, the myth was maintained that farm colonies would eventually attain self-sufficiency, and considerable discrepancies are apparent between euphoric public claims and actual cost figures. This led Johnstone (1906, p. 239) to observe: "The farm colony idea with a reasonable number of paid employees and a large extent of farm land, has made many institutions much nearer self-support, but still the per capita cost is over one hundred dollars per annum. Many of us have hitched our wagons to this star, but the millenium cometh not yet" (Johnstone, 1906, p. 239). He also objected to the continuing enlargement of institutions (e.g., 1908, 1913) and argued for some semblance of humanizing treatment of the retarded generally: "I have not gotten beyond the five or six hundred mark as yet. From an economical standpoint, I believe about 750 would be the most desirable size. I have argued against a large number being placed in one institution for that reason. If the institution is not very large, we get good classes. When we put men in one institution, women in another, and children in another, are we not taking away entirely the family idea?" (1913, p. 40).

Johnstone can be seen as "least extreme," but as far as opposition to the *principle* of segregation was concerned, there was absolutely none from the professional ranks: "We must beware of assuming universal consent because no serious note of opposition has been heard" (Johnson, 1903, p. 245). Personally, I found it both instructive and depressing that between about 1890 and 1918, I found not a single speaker or writer in opposition to the prevailing views of retarded people as a sinister menace. It made me wonder what nonexisting voice future reviewers will seek for our own epoch.

FAILURE TO SUPPORT COMMUNITY ALTERNATIVES TO SEGREGATION

The workers in the field painted themselves into a corner by advocating a practically unfeasible, scientifically invalid, and sociopolitically unacceptable policy of segregation while systematically rejecting alternative provisions such as education and family support.

During the alarmist period, education was no longer seen as effective in diminishing the degree of a person's retardation, and was not believed to prevent a retarded person's depravity: "When the state has taken the imbecile, and by training has brought out the best there is in him, when it has corrected his faults, so far as education can do it, when it has possibly taught him to read and write, to be more engaging in his manners and more attractive in appearance and bearing, and then has discharged him with his inherent defects in no way removed, to marry and perpetuate his kind, has it really done a commendable deed?" (Wilmarth, 1902, p. 159).

Thus, education came to be viewed as worthless. Rogers (1898), superintendent of Faribault (Minn.), questioned: "Does the Education of the Feeble-minded Pay?," and Johnson (1899, pp. 228-229) stated: "We made a mistake in keeping many children in school too long and taking them farther than they will have any need for." Bernstein (1913, p. 59) observed: "The patients who give us the most trouble are the ones who have been taught to read and write. They are always looking for an opportunity to send out a letter or note secretly, and give us trouble in other ways as well. If they could not write, much of the disturbance would be eliminated."

Even special education in the community, far from being seen primarily as a constructive and viable alternative, was seized upon as a means of identifying the retarded for subsequent institutionalization: "If . . . the special schools were so conducted as to constitute clearing houses to separate the inherently feeble-minded from those whose mental growth is retarded by circumstances temporary in character, they would serve a useful purpose; but if they are attempting the impossible, the education of the inherently feeble-minded to equip them to battle single-handed in the struggle for existence and thus prevent their entrance into institutions during their early years, they are harmful. It is our duty to point out the limitation of usefulness for such schools" (Murdoch, 1903, p. 71; similarly, 1909, pp. 65-66; Fitts, 1915; and Schlapp, 1915, p. 325). "The modern public school class for defective children ensures diagnosis and treatment at an early age, helps to inform the parents as to the dangers of mental defect, and admirably serves as a clearing house for permanent segregation, when necessary before adult life is reached. These classes should be established in every city and large town" (Fernald, 1915, p. 293).

Another community alternative that today strikes us as most progressive, *viz.*, the granting of a subsidy or "pension" to needy families with retarded persons in the household, was viciously attacked. Kentucky had had such a law since 1793 (Estabrook, 1928; Fernald, 1893), but superintendent Stewart from Kentucky (1894, p. 311) confessed that he was " . . . ashamed to tell you of our idiot law," and said that he had tried for 16 years to have the law repealed. He likened this law to the scalp law for foxes under which every fox scalp was rewarded with a $2.50 bounty until people took to raising foxes. "Now there is a premium offered for idiots." "The system is heinous" (Reports from States, 1890, p. 322). Dunlap (1899) also expressed disapproval of the pension law, and Estabrook (1928) suggested that it be repealed and the money used to enlarge the institution instead!

Finally, even the newly developing psychological community clinics were interpreted as agencies of the eugenic work (e.g., see *Journal of Psycho-Asthenics,* 1913, *18,* 13) rather than of community assistance.

THE END OF THE INDICTMENT

The peak of the indictment period was between about 1908 and 1912. By about 1920, workers in the field began to recognize two facts. Firstly, studies of the community adjustment of the retarded showed that they were not the menace as had been thought; and secondly, it was realized that the aims of segregation could not be achieved. One of the first major admissions of the failure of both sterilization *and* segregation took place in an address by Taft (1918), who commented: " . . . when by segregation we mean a fairly complete shutting off from society of all the feeble-minded, including the higher grade types, we ignore a profound aversion on the part of people in general to confinement for life for any human being, particularly when no offense has been committed commensurate with such punishment and when the individual to be segregated seems to the ordinary observer not to be very different from himself. This, combined with the feeling which relatives, particularly of the high grade feeble-minded have against segregation, makes any very complete program of this kind quite impossible for some time to come" (p. 545).

As early as 1915, Fernald (p. 296) had observed that "the courts are seldom willing to utilize even existing commitment laws without the consent of the parents, except in extreme cases." Perhaps the only justification for naming Howe's original institution for the Great Indictor himself is that Fernald, in the last years of his life, reversed himself, first in a celebrated speech in 1917. In 1919, he said: "The average citizen is not yet convinced that he should be taxed to permanently support an individual who is capable of thirty, fifty or seventy percent of normal economic efficiency, on the mere theory that he is more likely than a normal individual to become a social problem" (pp. 119-120; see also Fernald, 1924). "In practice, it has been found very difficult to ensure life-long segregation of the average moron. The courts are as ready to release the defective as they are to commit him in the first place. However proper and desirable it may be in theory to ensure the life-long segregation of large numbers of the moron class, it is a fact that there is a deep-seated prejudice on the part of lawyers, judges, and legislators toward assuming in advance that every moron will necessarily and certainly misbehave to an extent that he should be deprived of his liberty. That such misgivings are well-founded is apparently shown by the studies made of discharged patients at Rome and Waverly. At Waverly, a careful study of the discharges for twenty-five years showed that a very small proportion of the discharged male morons had committed crimes, or had married or become parents, or had failed to support themselves, or had become bad citizens." "We have begun to recognize the fact that there are good morons and bad morons, . . . " (pp. 119-120). After hearing Fernald in 1917, Murdock (1917, p. 41) said: " . . . the pendulum . . . had gone too far and is coming back."

"It is a matter of history that the two principal measures of social control in which main reliance was placed, during this period of alarm, for coping with the problem of mental deficiency, namely, sterilization and segregation, have failed to meet the situation as completely as the proponents of these measures had expected" (Davies, 1930, p. 130).

Taft (1918) proposed a new alternative to the field: identification, supervision, and control of the retarded in the community. This, it was widely felt, required that all the retarded be registered (Hasting, 1918), and there was widespread agitation to accomplish this. Fernald had advocated such registries all his career (for partially different reasons), but now the idea found new support, although to no avail.

The 1930 White House Conference on Child Health and Protection proposed a three-stage program to attack the problem of retardation. Stage one was identification and registration; stage two was divided into training of some and segregation of others; and stage three involved supervision, or, as it was frequently referred to, "social control," of retarded persons in the community. Registration was the key to the entire program. A most prominent text of the period between the alarmist one and the new enlightenment of the 1950's was *Social Control of the Mentally Deficient* (Davies, 1923, 1930).

Today, of course, we know that most retarded adults make an adequate adjustment in the community, and that they are more likely to be the victims rather than the perpetrators of social injustice. It is also widely accepted that heredity is a relatively insignificant factor in the causation of retardation, as compared to maternal health and socio-cultural factors.

MOMENTUM WITHOUT RATIONALES

We are now coming to another crucial point in this exposition. We cannot understand the institution, as we know it today, with all its objectionable features, unless we realize whence it came. I propose that essentially, many of our institutions, to this very day, operate in the spirit of 1925 when inexpensive segregation of a scarcely human retarded was seen as the only feasible alternative to combat a social menace. I am not proposing that this view is still held; I am proposing that most institutions function *as if* this view were still held. I will try to explain this hypothesis.

From 1847 to about 1925, institutions had evolved dynamically as ideas and innovations followed each other continuously. We can now judge the ideas faulty and the innovations as ineffective in achieving goals, but the force and dynamism of the institutional development cannot be denied. By 1925, however, a curious situation had developed. Essentially, the large institution, built for the ages, remote from population and teaching centers, was bereft of rationales. The only major rationale left was relief for hard-pressed families of the retarded, and if this rationale had been taken seriously it would have called either for community services, and/or for specialized and dispersed residential units of a more humanizing character, and nearer to population centers. Furthermore, the institutions were so crowded that it might have taken a decade without any admissions at all to reduce residents to an appropriate number.

If the field had continued to evolve as logically as it had until about 1925, it is clear that community and special residential services would have been developed, and institutions of the type we still have with us today would have withered away. However, community services did not develop fast enough, and this is probably one of the major reasons institutions did not change. Why these community services failed to develop is not simple to answer. I propose that four reasons may be paramount:

1. The professionals had indoctrinated the populace for about 30 years regarding the menace of retardation, and were to continue to assert the unchangeability of intelligence for another 30 years; thus, probably only a prolonged campaign of attitude modification (as finally developed in about 1950) could have secured community services.

2. Partially because of the pessimism communicated by the workers in the field, the interests of professionals became attracted to the new discoveries and increasing treatment opportunities in the area of mental health. A change in orientation of the National Conference on Charities and Correction reflected and/or contributed toward this trend. One of the organizers of this body in 1874 had been H. B. Wilbur, a pioneer in mental retardation. For almost a half century, the Conference was one of the major meeting grounds between professionals in the field of mental retardation and other professionals and public officials. In 1917, the name was changed to the Na-

tional Conference of Social Work; it became more of an association for one particular profession rather than a meeting ground and forum for many; and as papers on mental health and hygiene increased in frequency, papers on mental retardation began to diminish and eventually disappear.

3. The depression stifled progress in the development of social services other than those considered essential to economic survival of the nation, and mental retardation services are generally given low priority even when times are good.

4. World War II further diverted popular attention and concern. It is noteworthy that the "new look" in retardation began in about 1950 when there was prosperity and when war-related problems, such as demobilization, reintegration of veterans, and housing shortages, were finally being solved.

Any "institution" (in the sociological sense) that has much momentum but no viable rationale is likely to strive for self-perpetuation on the basis of its previous rationales and practices. And this is what I believe to have happened to our institutions (in the conventional sense). But 40 years of not thinking about our institutional models, and of model muddle (Wilkins, 1965), is enough! Let us consider only the following aspects that the institutional movement of today shares with the past, although these aspects no longer have viable rationales:

1. Large older institutions being further enlarged.

2. New institutions designed to be large, i.e., for more than 600-1,000 residents.

3. New institutions placed in inconvenient or remote locations.

4. Perpetuation of the omnibus (rather than specialization) concept of institutional purpose.

5. Uncritical and poorly rationalized intake practices; for instance, one need consider only the large number of young children with Down's Syndrome from adequate families that are accepted, often in infancy or from birth.

6. Continuation of dehumanization, despite the unprecedented move throughout the country toward increase in personal rights, equal protection under the law, distribution of affluence, better opportunities for the disadvantaged, etc. We have seen this concern expressed in civil rights laws, controversy over draft laws and the Vietnam war, definition of students' rights, reformulation of the rights of the accused, and the revision of the codes of ethics of many major professional societies. We are only beginning to see this concern extended to the retarded.

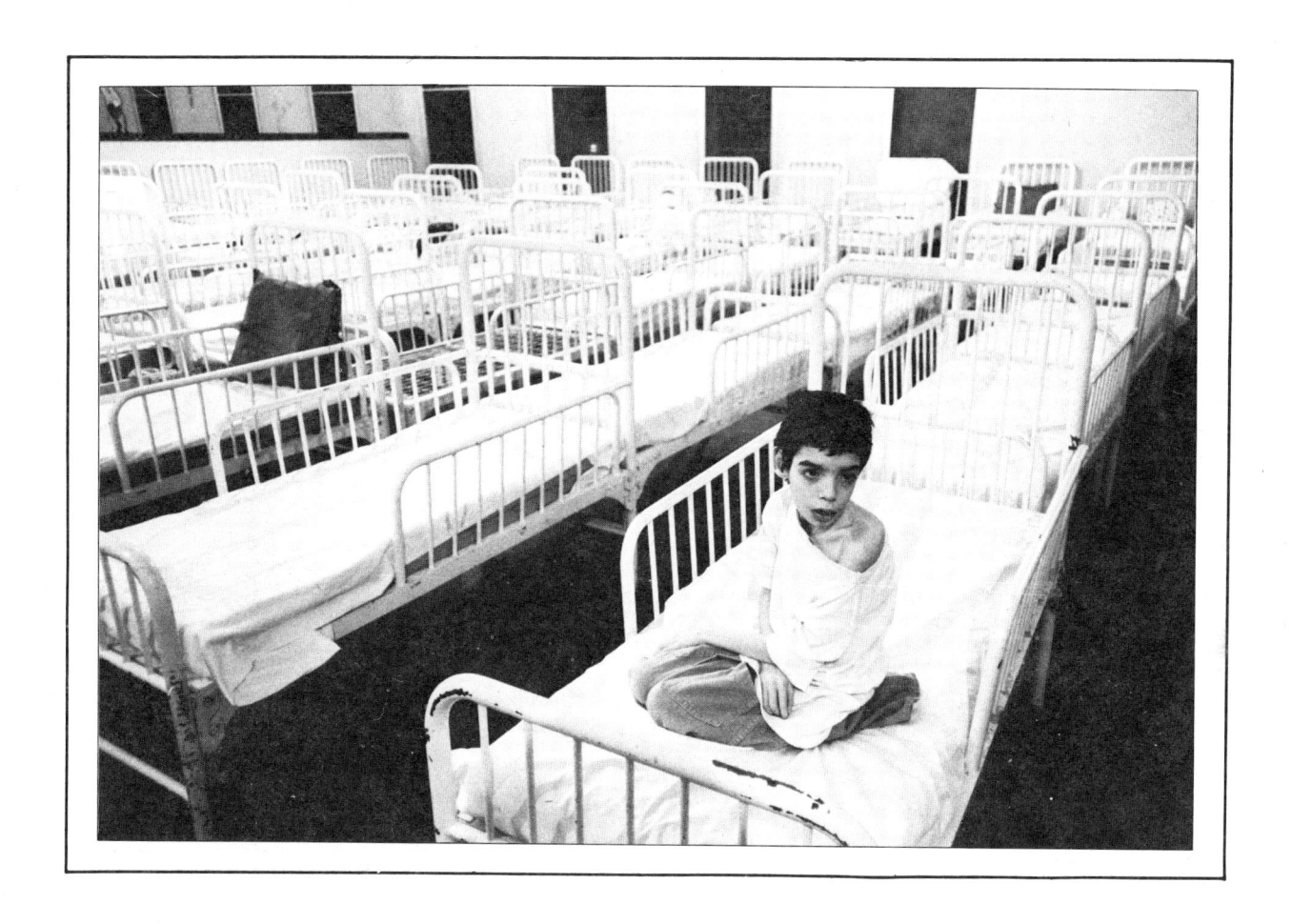

"Let us consider the aspects that the institutional movement of today shares with the past . . ."
(1970)

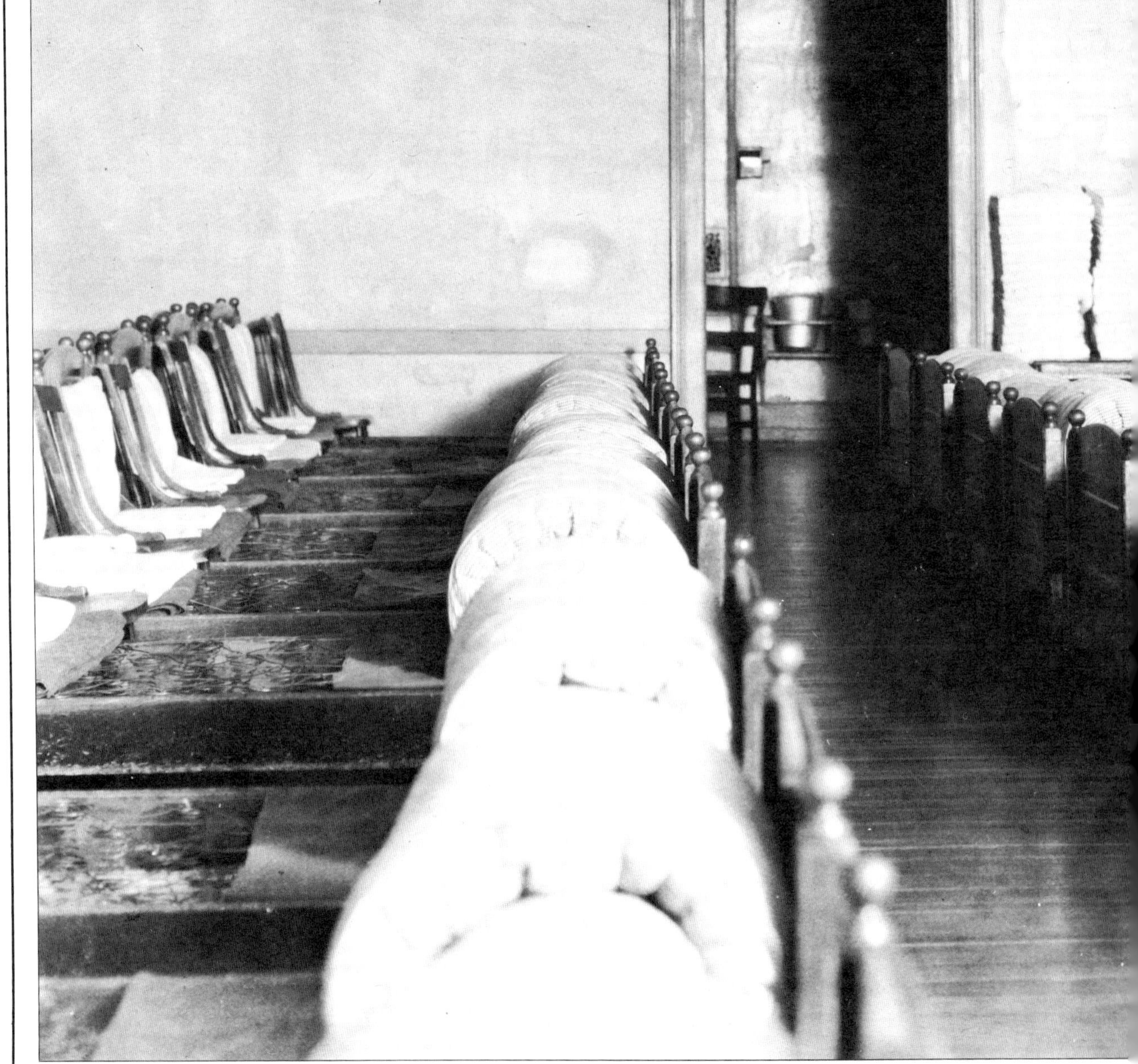

Chapter 3
The Realities of Institutional Accomplishments

The piles of towels, the barren metal hooks, the buckets used as toilets, the mattresses rolled, the pillows strapped to the bedboards in this scene show how the institution came to serve the needs of those who kept order. (1925)

If we compare the rationales for institution building with the realities of institution accomplishments, we can see that few of the hoped-for aims have even been approximated; that none of the major rationales advanced for institution building and institution running has held up; and that virtually every novel concept in institutional care was perverted eventually.

1. The schools became asylums, and small family residences became regimented institutions. Most of the retarded placed in these institutions were not made nondeviant; to the contrary: placement more often resulted in systematic "dehabilitation" (Sharman, 1966) which accentuated deviancy. This was only to be expected since any agency designed for the keeping of large numbers of deviant persons can ill afford to tolerate nondeviance in its midst, as illustrated by an experience of Fernald's: "I would like to ask the members of the Association what experience they have had in paying imbecile help. We have not done that very much, except in one or two cases. We had a very good driver who had been with us a few years; some suggested that we pay him ten cents a week; in the course of a month or two he thought he should have twenty-five cents, and so on to exorbitant ideas of his value, and such stretches of discipline and disobedience, that the only way to get him back to his tracks again was to put him back in the ranks" (Fernald in the discussion of Osborne, 1891, p. 181). "... *The social integration of the subnormal . . . is never feasible if society does not permit the subnormal to reach this integration*" (Speyer, 1963, p. 162), and the institution did "... not provide an accurate model of the society to which some of the retarded will eventually need to adjust" (Kirkland, 1967, p. 5).

2. The institution became not a paradise but a purgatory, not a Garden of Eden but an agency of dehumanization; to this day, residents are subjected to physical and mental abuse, to neglect and inadequate care and services, to environmental deprivation, and to restriction of the most basic rights and dignities of a citizen.

In 1886, Kerlin (p. 294) had a vision of what was to become the institution at Faribault, Minnesota: " ... we turn most approvingly to Minnesota's noble offering for this charity. Located on the beautiful bluff on Straight River, Faribault, with a singularly attractive country adjacent, exciting the kindliest interest of an intelligent and warm-hearted community, and with every advantage of space, fertility of soil, and amplitude of water, we know of no institution in the United States so happily and wisely begun. In fact, like the noble state itself, this institution is only embarrassed by the richness of its opportunities." And how does Faribault of today compare with this earlier vision of it?

Sonoma State Hospital in California was born in a similar vision: "The tract of land selected lies in the beautiful valley of Sonoma. It ... embraces over 1,600 acres. It is watered by three living streams, two of which rise on the place and give us 100,000 gallons of water daily, at an elevation of 150 feet above the building site. There are over 50,000 fruit-trees on the place, besides acres of vines and hundreds of acres of pasturage. Two railroads pass through the land, and will give us stations on it. The climate is perfect, the situation picturesque, the location central; and, altogether, the trustees are jubilant, and feel that the millenium is at hand. There seems no reason why our Home should not be the equal of any institution in the land. We shall not be satisfied with any lesser glory" (Murdock, 1889, p. 316).

> "In mountain heights, past stream and plain,
> And by the redwoods forests' sweep.
> In this broad land a spot is found,
> Aye! call it ever hallowed ground."
> (Osborne, 1891, p. 175).

Could anyone believe that this hallowed Garden of Eden became the Institution for 3,400 in which, according to a prominent visitor from abroad (Bank-Mikkelsen) residents were treated worse than in any institution he had seen in a dozen countries and, indeed, worse than cattle are permitted to be treated in Denmark (*Children Limited,* Dec. 1967, p. 2). Or that a mother preferred that her child die rather than live at Sonoma? (Anonymous, 1968).

In 1901, an observer remarked that the retarded in a certain Midwestern institution were being herded like so many cattle (Clark, 1901). Sixty-eight years later, the residents were still being herded like cattle in the same institution in that cattle-oriented state. How many more years?

A 1787 visitor at Pennsylvania Hospital, the first U.S. public institution to receive the mentally afflicted for treatment, saw naked residents bedded in straw, in locked, underground dungeonlike cells that had small windows for passing food, and he exclaimed in seeming self-satisfaction that " . . . every possible relief is afforded them in the power of man," rejoicing in " . . . the pleasing evidence of what humanity and benevolence can do . . . " (Deutsch, 1949, p. 62). Deutsch also described a case cited by Dorothea Dix in 1847, in which a harmless deranged person was kept summer and winter in an open pen. He was fed hog slop and kept on straw which was changed every two weeks in summer, less often in winter. He was exposed to rain, heat, cold, and snow, and his feet had frozen off into shapeless stumps. The keepers of this wretch, however, saw themselves as offering kindly treatment.

Today, all of us see the inhumanity of such treatments, because our values have grown. But some of us do not see the 1968 equivalents of the 1787 and 1847 treatments, or of the keepers' responses. Are not, in 1968, denial of property rights, or human contacts and perceptual stimulation; restriction of movement and communication; denial of wages for work; compulsion to use nonprivate toilets; denial of the privilege to wear clothes; behavior control by means of medication rather than education or guidance; enforced idleness; and innumerable other practices common in our institutions the equivalents of the inhumane practices of 1787 and 1847? Are not the rationalizations of these 1968 practices equivalent to the protestations advanced by the keepers of 1787 and 1847? How will the professionals and public of 2068 judge them?

3. Institutional segregation did not contribute much to prevention of retardation, and the devalued retarded person is still with us. Indeed, there is reason to believe that with the increasing complexity of life, the number of persons who will fail to meet societal demands will increase.

4. Institutionalization was not accomplished inexpensively, as had been claimed. The concentration of residents in large institutions has, in most cases, been more costly than provision of community services would have been. Work, first rationalized as constructive occupation, became exploitation as cost cutting became important and, again contrary to claim, only a modest number of the retarded became self-sufficient in the institution. Those retarded residents who did become good workers began to replace institution employees and thus became too valuable to be released; the institution could not have functioned without unpaid captive labor. To save money, the large solid multi-purpose (usually original) building of the institution was permitted to become an overcrowded dungeon; "cottages" conceived to replace them became large overcrowded buildings, sometimes housing 200 residents and their attendants (Bliss, 1913); the "plain, substantial buildings" designed to reduce expenses became bare, vast mausoleums; and the colonies which were to relieve institutions of their crowdedness, bring about more humane living conditions, and reduce costs became large institutions in their own right.

5. The concentration of skilled expert staff never materialized, one of the main reasons being the partially self-elected isolation of institutions remote from centers of learning and population. To the contrary, institutions have tended to act as sieves, retaining professionals who are deviant themselves, and passing on the others to universities and community programs. The unlicensed physician, often unable to communicate in English, is notorious, as are professionals who are alcoholic, drug addicted, unstable, or health-handicapped. While it is desirable to find niches for such individuals, it is significant that such persons should have become concentrated in our institutions. Professionals not good enough to work on us or our normal children were, it seems, good

enough to work on someone else's retarded children. Employees, as much as residents, become "institutionalized" (Cleland & Peck, 1967).

To this day, staffing is a dilemma in both rural and urban locations. Recruiting for nonprofessional personnel is usually easier in rural locations unacceptable to many professionals. Professionals are easier to attract into urban locations, but there, nonprofessional turnover may run 50 per cent a year, even with relatively good salaries (e.g., Jaslow, Kime & Green, 1966). The very heterogeneity of residents, desired by many workers in the field, has presented a major problem in staffing because so many different skills and types of training are needed to serve a group with a tremendous variety of problems (Jaslow, Kime & Green, 1966).

6. From the beginning, and ever since, the research potential of institutions has been exalted (e.g., Seguin, 1870; Kerlin, 1885; Sprattling, 1903; Johnson, 1904; Schlapp, 1915), and one of the arguments for congregating large numbers of residents had been that this would facilitate research. This potential has never been fulfilled except at a very few institutions at a given time. Even today, with over 150 institutions, less than a half-dozen can be said to be making a well-sustained, active, and significant research contribution to the field.

7. One goal was often achieved by institutions: providing relief to families. But even here we have an element of irony in that family relief could often have been achieved better and cheaper by other measures than institutionalization.

If my formulations and interpretations are correct, we can summarize the trends in United States residential services to the retarded as follows, and as depicted in Figure 1. Attitudes toward retardation paralleled those toward a number of other deviancies. Around 1850, a developmentally oriented residential model attempted to return deviant people to the community. Between 1870 and 1890, this model was replaced with one based on pity which called for protective isolation of the retarded. This period was brief, and was soon succeeded by one emphasizing the menacing nature of deviancy. Certain trends that had originated during the pity period were accentuated, so that the retarded were congregated into huge groups, sequestrated from society, segregated from other retarded persons of the opposite sex, asexualized, and dehumanized in poorly supported, inhumanely run regimented institutions. The puzzling and anachronistic mode of functioning of today's institutions can be understood if we see them as having been maintained by a tremendous amount of momentum but bereft of rationales for about 40 years.

I submit that the problem of residential services cannot be solved by working on a number of specifics at a time, or by calling for simple-minded, low-level measures such as more money. All the money in the world will not change the minds of men. What we need are concepts and models. The current model, the entire system, as Howe called it, is inconsistent with contemporary cultural values and scientific knowledge. We need a model of services that is appropriate to knowledge, resources, and needs of the 1970's and beyond, and that is based on a contemporary perception of the nature and role of the retarded person in our society. Such new and viable ideology (e.g., the principle of normalization) is gaining wide acceptance. With the acceptance of this new ideology, we are witnessing the agonized death struggle of an institution model based on a perception of the retarded as a menace and/or subhuman organism.

The greatest irony lies in the fact that the founding fathers foresaw much of what happened, and repudiated the trend institutions were taking within 20 years of their founding. H. B. Wilbur (1879) stated that he had always been in favor of building specialized institutions rather than enlarging existing ones for multiple purposes. In 1866, Howe gave the dedication speech for a new institution for the blind in Batavia, New York. The fact that he virtually repudiated this institution at its very beginning, and as the guest of honor, cannot be overemphasized, as it constituted an act of incredible courage and conviction. Everything he said applies to the institutions for

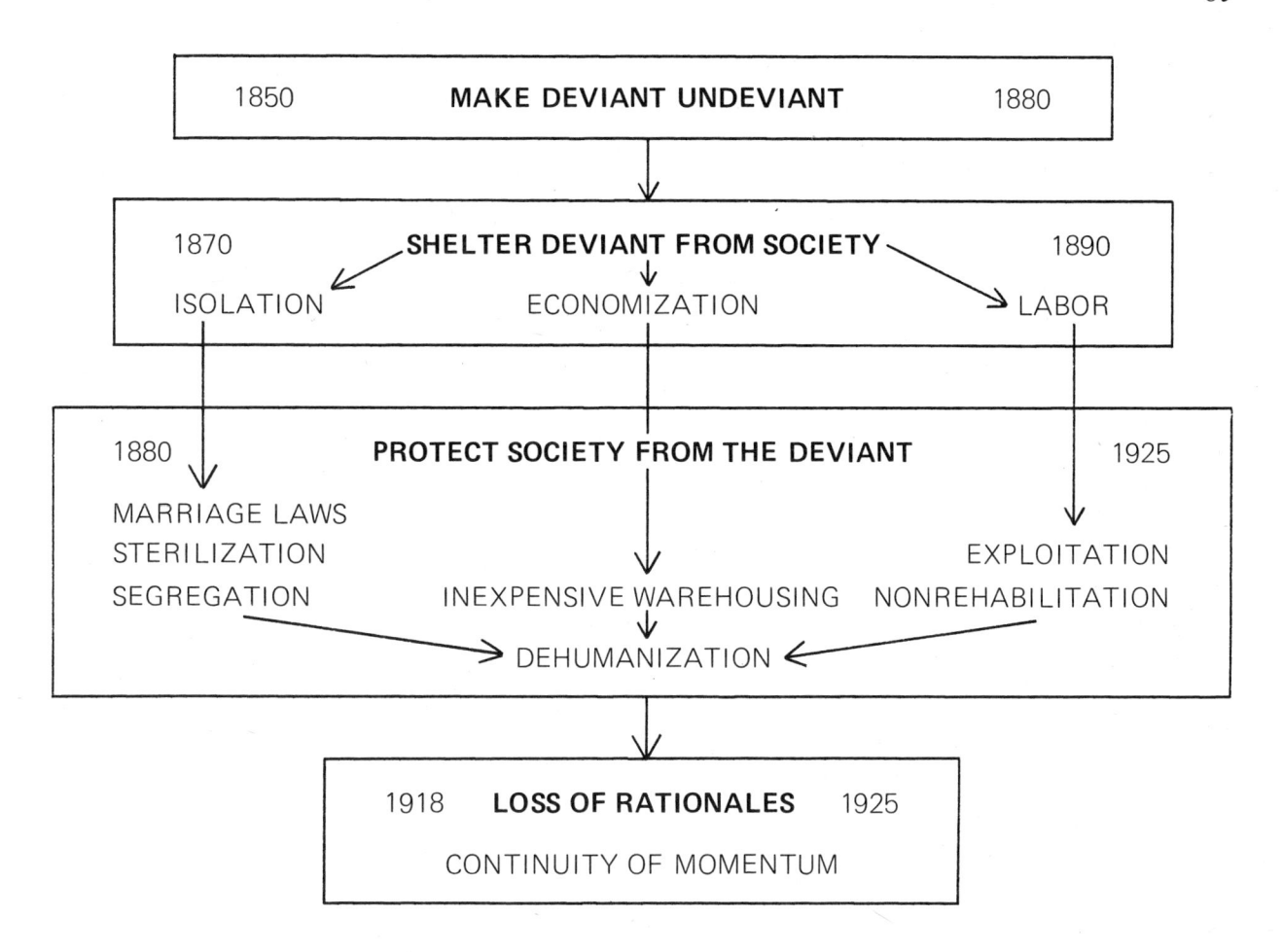

FIGURE 1: Graphic Summarization of the Evolution of Institutional Rationales and Practices.

the retarded as well.

"As it is with individuals, so it is with communities; and society moved by pity for some special form of suffering, hastens to build up establishments which sometimes increase the very evil which it wishes to lessen.

"There are several such already in this country; and unless we take heed there will be many more. Our people have rather a passion for public institutions, and when their attention is attracted to any suffering class, they make haste to organize one for its benefit.

"But instead of first carefully inquiring whether an institution is absolutely necessary, that is, whether there is no more natural and effectual manner of relieving the class; and afterwards, taking care that no vicious principle be incorporated into the establishment; they hastily build a great showy building, and gather within its walls a crowd of persons of like condition or infirmity; and organize a community where everything goes by clock-work and steam. If there be a vicious principle in the organization, as of closely associating persons who ought to live apart, it is forgotten in admiration of contrivances for making steam do what once was done by the good housewife, with her cook and maid; and of the bright coppers, the garish walls, and the white floors.

"But no steam power, no human power can long keep a vicious principle from cropping out. It has done so in many European institutions of charity; it will do so in many of ours" (pp. 18-19).

" . . . Grave errors were incorporated into the very organic principles of our institutions . . . which make them already too much like asylums; which threaten to cause real asylums to grow out of them, and to engender other evils. Let me set forth a little my idea of the general principles which should underlie all such establishments, and which have been too much neglected in the organization of many of our public institutions.

"All great establishments in the nature of boarding schools, where the sexes must be separated; where there must be boarding in common, and sleeping in congregate dormitories; where there must be routine, and formality, and restraint, and repression of individuality; where the charms and refining influences of the true family relation cannot be had, — all such institutions are unnatural, undesirable, and very liable to abuse. We should have as few of them as is possible, and those few should be kept as small as possible.

"The human family is the unit of society. The family, as it was ordained by our Great Father, with its ties with kith and kin; with its tender associations of childhood and youth; with its ties of affection and of sympathy; with its fireside, its table, and its domestic altar, — there is the place for the early education of the child. His instruction may be had in school; his heart and character should be developed and moulded at home.

"Artificial families have been tried and found wanting. Communities in imitation of the natural family, especially those confined to one sex, are fertile of evil. Witness the old nunneries and monasteries, darkened and saddened by lack of the sunlight of affection and love; embittered by petty passions and strife; soured by crushed hopes and yearnings; and defiled by unnatural vices. Witness soldiers in detached garrisons, sailors on long voyages; prisoners under long sentences. Wherever there must be separation of the sexes, isolation from society, absence of true family relation, and monotony of life, there must come evils of various kinds, which no watchfulness can prevent, and physician can cure.

"We should be cautious about establishing such artificial communities, or those approaching them in character, for any children and youth; but more especially should we avoid them for those who have natural infirmity; or any marked peculiarity of mental organization.

"Let me dwell upon this, for in my view, it is very important. Such persons spring up sporadically in the community, and they should be kept diffused among sound and normal persons. Separation, and not congregation, should be the law of their treatment; for out of their infirmity or abnormality there necessarily grow some abnormal and undesirable effects, and unless these be counteracted by education, they disturb the harmonious developments of character. These effects are best counteracted by bringing up the child among ordinary children, and subjecting him to ordinary social and family influences; but, on the contrary, they are intensified by constant and close association with children who are marked by the same infirmity or peculiarity . . . . We should therefore keep this truth in mind; and give it due weight when forming plans for the treatment of any special class of persons.

"As much as may be, surround insane and excitable persons with sane people, and ordinary influences; vicious children with virtuous people and virtuous influences; blind children with those who see; mute children with those who speak; and the like.

"People run counter to this principle for the sake of economy, and of some other good end, which they suppose cannot be had in any other way; as when they congregate the insane in hospitals, vicious children in reformatories, criminals in prisons, paupers in almshouses, orphans in asylums, blind children and mute children in boarding schools. Hence I begin to consider such eatablishments as evils which must be borne with, for the time, in order to obviate greater evils. I would take heed, however, against multiplying them unnecessarily. I would keep them as small as I could. I would take the most stringent measurements for guarding against those undesirable effects which lessen their usefulness; and for dispensing with as many of them as may be possible.

"But, besides this general objection to such establishments, there is another and more practical objection to the method of congregating . . . any class of young persons marked by an infirmity like deafness or blindness. They depend more than ordinary persons do for their happiness and for their support upon the ties of kindred, of friendship, and of neighborhood. All these, therefore, ought' to be nourished and strengthened during childhood and youth—for it is then, and then only, that they take such deep root as to become strong, and life-lasting. — The home of the blind and of the mute should be his native town or village; there, if possible, he should live during childhood and youth; there he should form his friendships; there, if he comes to need special aid it will be given most readily and fitly; and there his old age will be cherished. — Beware how you needlessly sever any of those ties of family, of friendship, of neighborhood, *during the period of their strongest growth,* lest you make a homeless man, a wanderer and a stranger. Especially beware how you cause him to neglect forming early relations of affection with those whose sympathy and friendship will be most important to him during life, to wit, those who have all their senses; and how you restrict him to such relations with persons subject to an infirmity like his own.

"I would observe, by the way, that the necessity now felt for a new institution in your state has arisen, partly at least, from radical faults in the organization of the old one, which necessarily led to faults in its administration such as I have noticed. If the conditions of admission had been such as to exclude some who entered, but who ought not to have entered; if stringent measures had been taken to prevent the multiplication of graduates in and about the institution, and to encourage their dispersion and settlement in the several towns, instead of leaving them to congregate in the commercial capital, and to besiege the political capital; if these things had been done, the state would perhaps not now be called upon to incur the cost of building and the continual expense of carrying on a second institution.

"But, it is settled that you are to have one, and, I trust, it will become worthy of the generous motives which prompt its erection; and of the great state which is to build it.

"Take heed that it shall be organized on sound principles; and while copying all the good features of existing institutions, avoid those which are not good. Those establishments are all faulty. Not one of them is worthy to be your model in all respects; and the persons who flatter themselves that their favorite one is worthy to be copied exactly, are blind to faults which can be seen by looking beneath the surface. Never mind their showy buildings and special accommodations; you may as well measure the morality of a family

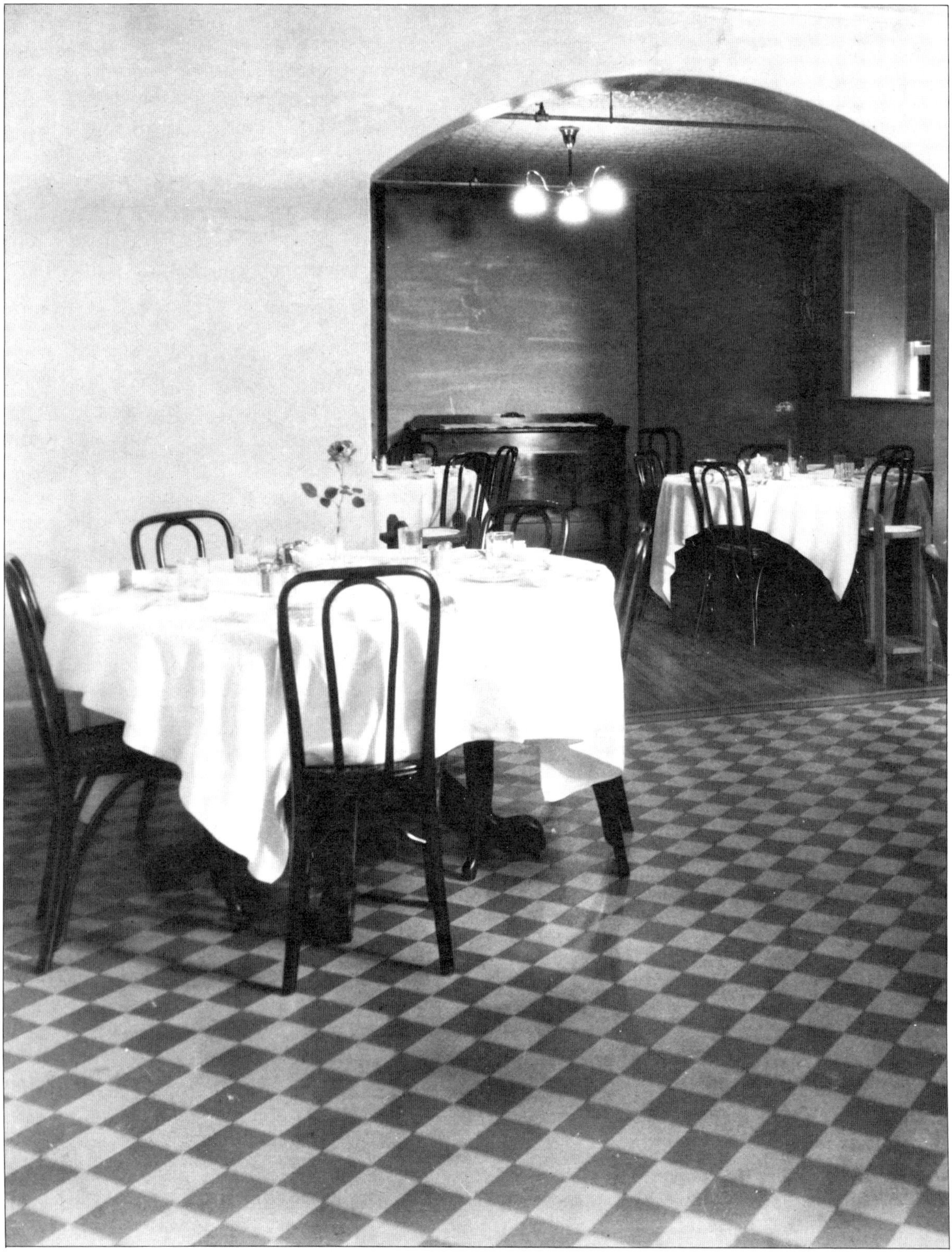

The staff not only ate apart from the residents, they did so in very different dining rooms. Notice the table cloths, linen napkins, tables for six, glasses, vases and decorative flooring. (1925)

In contrast, the residents ate in larger rooms, on barren tables for 16 people each, bare floors, no cane back chairs, and a place setting consisting of one tablespoon, a mug, and one soup bowl. (1925)

by the structure and arrangement of its dwelling-house, as test institutions by their mechanical advantages; but look at the principles and system by which they are conducted. You will, then, find they are faulty in many respects.

"They are generally wrong in receiving pupils too indiscriminately; being, in most cases, tempted to do so by the fact that they are paid according to the number they receive. They are wrong in receiving all pupils as boarders, when they should receive those only who cannot board at home, or in private families. They are wrong in associating the blind too closely, and too many years together; thus loosening or breaking the ties of family and of neighborhood, — segregating them from society, — forming a class apart, — creating a feeling of caste, — and so intensifying all the unfavorable effects growing out of the infirmity of blindness . . . They are creating the necessity, or the demand, for permanent life asylums; all of which consummations are devoutly to be prayed against.

"Instead, then, of copying the existing institution, I think, that in organizing a new one something like the following rough plan should be adopted: — If the field were all clear, and no buildings provided, there should be built only a building for school-rooms, recitation rooms, music rooms and work shops; and *these should be in or near the centre of a dense population.* For other purposes, ordinary houses would suffice" (Howe, 1866, pp. 39-43).

Howe also repudiated the trend from education to pity: " . . . aid should not be given in alms, or in any way that savors of alms. Were it possible for government to pension every blind person for life, that would probably do more harm than good. We are safe in saying that as far as possible, they should be considered and treated just as ordinary persons, our equals and friends, are treated, and not singled out as special objects of pity. This is too often forgotten" (Howe, 1866, p. 37).

When I read these passages, I was astonished. Howe had truly " . . . dipt into the future, far as human eye could see, saw the visions of the world, and all the wonders that would be" (Tennyson). It was as if the founder himself was saying: "Stop it, you fools; we have made a gigantic error!" Alas, Howe had been 100 years ahead of his time, and his cautions went unheeded.

Seguin is probably the best-known figure in mental retardation in this country. He was brought by Howe from France, was instrumental in the founding of about a half-dozen of our early institutions, and was cofounder and first president of what is now the American Association on Mental Deficiency. Yet Seguin (1870), too, disapproved of the trend of things in 1869, and of the developing isolation of the institutions. " . . . In locating these schools through the country . . . " they have put them out of the reach of concourse of scientific men and means, which are concentrated in capital cities" (p. 43). "This necessity of the situation—for, if these institutions do not progress, they will retrograde—demands of the selection of a suitable place among scientific surroundings; the direction of a man who understands the philoaophy of the labor, the selection of microscopists, anatomists, psychologists, young medical men eager for study, devoted women ready to teach, to nurse, and to acquire the capacities so much wanted in other schools. With this force at command, there will be treated, besides the question directly relating to idiocy and medicine, those which touch society through education. It is not a minute too soon.

"From all the points of the compass, steam and electricity accumulate men and ideas on this continent that will soon be, for good or evil, *the new world,* new for evil if the comers invade us, not by the sword, but their low spirit of submission to Eastern or Western bonzes; new for good, if we are ready, with a powerful physiological system of education, to assimilate them, women, men, children, of all races and colors, to our unity and independence" (p. 44).

In 1878, Seguin added: " . . . if ideas create architecture, architecture reacts upon its mother-idea, to develop, distort, even kill it (as it appears by the influence that the latter form of the insane asylum has exercised on the theory and practice of the treatment of insanity). Truly, the ideas, too soon cast in brick-form, shrink by compression; and the monument erected for their development becomes too often their empty sarcophagus" (p. 60).

Fifty years ago, Kirkbride (1916, p. 250) lamented, to little avail: "In studying the problems connected with the construction, organization and management of public institutions for defectives, I have had varying emotions . . . While I have seen much to thrill me and to make me proud of the devoted men and women who are giving their lives to the care of their less fortunate fellows, I have seen so much of the handicaps under which they suffer, resulting from mistakes in planning, construction and arrangement of the institutions in which they work, that my emotions have often been very mixed and sobering.

"Why, I have often asked myself, have the experiences, the failures and the successes of others not been of more use in preventing the needless repetition of costly mistakes? Local customs, politics, prejudice, lack of initiative, courage and vision, and a host of other factors are included in the answer."

The remarkable thing is that our experience has been shared by many countries that built large institutions in the last 100 years. It seems as if the very model, as we have known it, is unworkable.

If it is a universal fact that this model has failed, perhaps the institution built on it is not the solution to our problems. Perhaps the institution as we know it is unworkable and cannot be salvaged no matter how much money we spend.

In Greek mythology we encounter a somewhat overly friendly character by the name of Procrustes. He wanted very much to be a good host to weary warfarers, and when a traveler journeyed past his dwelling, Procrustes would insist that he stay the night with him. After some wining and dining, Procrustes would show his guest to his bed. Trouble was, there was only one bed, of one certain size, and Procrustes was a perfectionist. The bed just had to fit the guest. So if the guest was tall, Procrustes chopped off his legs until guest and bed were exactly of the same size. If the guest was too small, the host strapped him into a rack and lengthened him out a few inches. Obviously, by doing things his own way, Procrustes was prepared for all comers.

The moral of the parable: our institutions have been Procrustean. It did not matter who or what the resident was, whether young or old, whether borderline or profoundly retarded; whether physically handicapped or physically sound; whether deaf or blind; whether rural or urban; whether from the local town or from 500 miles away; whether well-behaved or ill-behaved. We took them all, by the thousands, 5,000 and 6,000 in some institutions. We had all the answers in one place, using the same facilities, the same personnel, the same attitudes, and largely the same treatment.

And if our guest did not fit, we made him fit!

What we need to do is take an entirely fresh look at the needs of the retarded, and increase the goodness of fit between their needs and our programs. And we must face the possibility that we may need a new bed.

Appendix 1

Maintenance costs for residents in United States public institutions for the mentally retarded, 1848-1966.

Beginning the section on "Protecting Deviant Individuals From Non-deviant Ones" and elaborated in the section on "Failure of Preventive Segregation," certain hypotheses were evolved regarding the relationship between institutional admission trends and institutional costs. To substantiate these hypotheses, I collated data on per capita maintenance costs of U.S. public institutions (or private institutions with a substantial proportion of publicly supported residents) for the mentally retarded between 1848 and 1966. In compiling these data, only operating expenses were listed. Where it was impossible to separate capital expenditures and operating expenses, no entry was made.

The data were derived from articles and "Reports from States" in the annual proceedings of the National Conference on Charities and in the various forerunners of the *American Journal on Mental Deficiency,* and from U.S. census and National Institute of Mental Health reports on institutions. In the U.S. censuses of 1850-1890, questions were asked aimed at the identification of retarded persons in the community. In 1880 and 1890, the Census Bureau reported data on residents in institutions for the retarded. Similar resident counts were published in 1906 and 1914, for the years 1903-1905 and 1909-1910 respectively. In 1919, reports on maintenance costs for the year 1915 were added to basic resident movement data. Similar data were published in 1926, 1931, 1932, 1934, 1935, 1936, 1937, 1938, 1939, 1941, 1943, and 1943 again, for years 1922, 1926-1927, 1928, 1929-1932, 1933, 1934, 1935, 1936, 1937, 1938, 1939, and 1940 respectively. In most but not all cases, maintenance costs for the retarded and epileptic were not reported separately, but since most epileptic residents appeared to be also retarded, this should have had little effect on overall trends.

The census-derived data reported here are somewhat at variance with those tabulated by Best (1965, p. 274) for the years 1922-1960. Apparently, Best combined maintenance and capital expenditure costs for some years, and costs for retarded and epileptic residents in years where a distinction between these was possible.

Cost data derived from noncensus sources are likely to contain some errors: (1) Such data were sometimes reported in informal conferences, or as estimates. (2) I computed some cost estimates indirectly by dividing total maintenance costs in a state as reported in one reference by the total number of institution residents for the same state and year as cited in another. (3) Early reports did not always make a distinction between costs and expenditures: since many residents were partially supported by fees and subsidies, the true costs were sometimes higher than the appropriated expenditures. (4) Early maintenance figures sometimes did not include some costs later subsumed under maintenance, such as clothes. However, most of these errors are likely to result in underestimates for the early years, and thus accentuate the trend this appendix is trying to document, *viz.*, the decline in expenditures from the early days of institutions to the end of the indictment period.

The cost data are presented in two tables. The first one breaks costs down by state between 1878 (when data apparently first began to be reported in national publications) and 1931. In some instances in Table 1, the figures apply only to one of several institutions within a state. The second table reports costs between 1926 and 1966 for the country as a whole because 1926 marked the beginning of annual nationwide cost surveys. In both tables, mean or median costs are listed both in reported dollar values, as well as in terms of 1967 dollar value equivalents as derived from cost of living indices. The reason for the conversion of costs into 1967 dollar values was to obtain a truer picture of cost trends. It should be pointed out, however, that the conversion has its shortcomings, and it is possible that the 1967 equivalents increasingly underestimate as one goes back in time. However, the general trends apparent in Figure 2 are probably valid. Finally, be it noted that crossed out spaces in Table 1 indicate that an institution did not exist in the year indicated.

A special word is in order on costs in Howe's institution, the first one to be publicly supported (Third and Final Report, 1852). Massachusetts granted $7,500 for a 3-year period, additional receipts being $3,808. Apparently, only a fraction of the total of 32 residents admitted were in residence more than one year. I would estimate from the somewhat vague wording of the report that the average daily census might have been 20. This means that annual per capita maintenance costs must have been about $188. Whether any of this was used for capital expenditure is doubtful, since in the transition from the experimental to the permanent phase of the institution, items that had been bought were sold again. Also, Howe (p. 21) clearly states that the money expended was equivalent to that required to teach "hundreds of children in the common schools."

TABLE I
Per Capita Maintenance Expenditures in United States Public Institutions for the Mentally Retarded, By State, for 1878 to 1931

	States	1878	1879	1880	1881	1882	1883	1884
1.	Alabama	xxxxxxxxxxxxxxxxxxxxxxxxxxxxxxxxxxxxxxxxxxxxxxxx						
2.	California	xxxxxxxxxxxxxxxxxxxxxxxxxxxxxxxxxxxxxxxxxxxxxxxx						
3.	Colorado	xxxxxxxxxxxxxxxxxxxxxxxxxxxxxxxxxxxxxxxxxxxxxxxx						
4.	Connecticut							129
5.	Delaware	xxxxxxxxxxxxxxxxxxxxxxxxxxxxxxxxxxxxxxxxxxxxxxxx						
6.	Dist. of Columbia	xxxxxxxxxxxxxxxxxxxxxxxxxxxxxxxxxxxxxxxxxxxxxxxx						
7.	Florida	xxxxxxxxxxxxxxxxxxxxxxxxxxxxxxxxxxxxxxxxxxxxxxxx						
8.	Illinois		240[3]					200
9.	Indiana	xxxxxx						
10.	Iowa							
11.	Kansas	xxxxxxxxxxxxxxxxx				159		250
12.	Kentucky							193
13.	Louisiana	xxxxxxxxxxxxxxxxxxxxxxxxxxxxxxxxxxxxxxxxxxxxxxxx						
14.	Maine	xxxxxxxxxxxxxxxxxxxxxxxxxxxxxxxxxxxxxxxxxxxxxxxx						
15.	Maryland	xxxxxxxxxxxxxxxxxxxxxxxxxxxxxxxxxxxxxxxxxxxxxxxx						
16.	Massachusetts							
17.	Michigan	xxxxxxxxxxxxxxxxxxxxxxxxxxxxxxxxxxxxxxxxxxxxxxxx						
18.	Minnesota	xxxxxx						
19.	Mississippi	xxxxxxxxxxxxxxxxxxxxxxxxxxxxxxxxxxxxxxxxxxxxxxxx						
20.	Missouri	xxxxxxxxxxxxxxxxxxxxxxxxxxxxxxxxxxxxxxxxxxxxxxxx						
21.	Nebraska	xxxxxxxxxxxxxxxxxxxxxxxxxxxxxxxxxxxxxxxxxxxxxxxx						
22.	New Hampshire	xxxxxxxxxxxxxxxxxxxxxxxxxxxxxxxxxxxxxxxxxxxxxxxx						
23.	New Jersey	xxxxxxxxxxxxxxxxxxxxxxxxxxxxxxxxxxxxxxxxxxxxxxxx						
24.	New York							
	a) Craig	xxxxxxxxxxxxxxxxxxxxxxxxxxxxxxxxxxxxxxxxxxxxxxxx						
	b) Newark		155					
	c) Rome	xxxxxxxxxxxxxxxxxxxxxxxxxxxxxxxxxxxxxxxxxxxxxxxx						
	d) Syracuse	167[4]	161	152				
25.	North Carolina	xxxxxxxxxxxxxxxxxxxxxxxxxxxxxxxxxxxxxxxxxxxxxxxx						
26.	North Dakota	xxxxxxxxxxxxxxxxxxxxxxxxxxxxxxxxxxxxxxxxxxxxxxxx						
27.	Ohio					165	166	165
28.	Oklahoma	xxxxxxxxxxxxxxxxxxxxxxxxxxxxxxxxxxxxxxxxxxxxxxxx						
29.	Oregon	xxxxxxxxxxxxxxxxxxxxxxxxxxxxxxxxxxxxxxxxxxxxxxxx						
30.	Pennsylvania			176				217[1]
								160[2]
31.	Rhode Island	xxxxxxxxxxxxxxxxxxxxxxxxxxxxxxxxxxxxxxxxxxxxxxxx						
32.	South Carolina	xxxxxxxxxxxxxxxxxxxxxxxxxxxxxxxxxxxxxxxxxxxxxxxx						
33.	South Dakota	xxxxxxxxxxxxxxxxxxxxxxxxxxxxxxxxxxxxxxxxxxxxxxxx						
34.	Texas	xxxxxxxxxxxxxxxxxxxxxxxxxxxxxxxxxxxxxxxxxxxxxxxx						
35.	Vermont	xxxxxxxxxxxxxxxxxxxxxxxxxxxxxxxxxxxxxxxxxxxxxxxx						
36.	Virginia	xxxxxxxxxxxxxxxxxxxxxxxxxxxxxxxxxxxxxxxxxxxxxxxx						
37.	Washington	xxxxxxxxxxxxxxxxxxxxxxxxxxxxxxxxxxxxxxxxxxxxxxxx						
38.	Wisconsin	xxxxxxxxxxxxxxxxxxxxxxxxxxxxxxxxxxxxxxxxxxxxxxxx						
39.	Wyoming	xxxxxxxxxxxxxxxxxxxxxxxxxxxxxxxxxxxxxxxxxxxxxxxx						
	Median	167	161	164	165	159	166	193
	Mean 1967 $ Value	702	685	689	668	621	689	843

[1] Higher functioning or colony resident only.
[2] Severely retarded only.
[3] Low estimate; exclusive of items such as clothing and building maintenance.
[4] Possibly a high estimate.

	1885	1886	1887	1888	1889	1890	1891	1892	1893	1894
1.	xxxxxxxxxxxxxxxxxxxxxxxxxxxxxxxxxxxxxxxxxxxxxxxxxxxxxxxxxxxxxx
2.				300	277			197	218	183
3.	xxxxxxxxxxxxxxxxxxxxxxxxxxxxxxxxxxxxxxxxxxxxxxxxxxxxxxxxxxxxxx
4.		130
5.	xxxxxxxxxxxxxxxxxxxxxxxxxxxxxxxxxxxxxxxxxxxxxxxxxxxxxxxxxxxxxx
6.	xxxxxxxxxxxxxxxxxxxxxxxxxxxxxxxxxxxxxxxxxxxxxxxxxxxxxxxxxxxxxx
7.	xxxxxxxxxxxxxxxxxxxxxxxxxxxxxxxxxxxxxxxxxxxxxxxxxxxxxxxxxxxxxx
8.		180						172		149
9.		127		120	109			182	181[3]	191
10.		163	156					161[3]	178	162
11.			214		184		175	174	171	140
12.				150	227					211
13.	xxxxxxxxxxxxxxxxxxxxxxxxxxxxxxxxxxxxxxxxxxxxxxxxxxxxxxxxxxxxxx
14.	xxxxxxxxxxxxxxxxxxxxxxxxxxxxxxxxxxxxxxxxxxxxxxxxxxxxxxxxxxxxxx
15.	xxxxxxxxxxxxxxxxxxxxxx						162	150	
16.	169	169[2]					167	158	157	140
17.	xxxxxxxxxxxxxxxxxxxxxxxxxxxxxxxxxxxxxxxxxxxxxxxx
18.				215		187		166	167	187
19.	xxxxxxxxxxxxxxxxxxxxxxxxxxxxxxxxxxxxxxxxxxxxxxxxxxxxxxxxxxxxxx
20.	xxxxxxxxxxxxxxxxxxxxxxxxxxxxxxxxxxxxxxxxxxxxxxxxxxxxxxxxxxxxxx
21.	xxxxxxxxxxxxxx					197	261	211[3]	151	
22.	xxxxxxxxxxxxxxxxxxxxxxxxxxxxxxxxxxxxxxxxxxxxxxxxxxxxxxxxxxxxxx
23.	xxxxxxxxxxxxxxxxxxxxxx								251
24.
a)	xxxxxxxxxxxxxxxxxxxxxxxxxxxxxxxxxxxxxxxxxxxxxxxxxxxxxxxxxxxxxx
b)				126			123	111		116
c)	xxxxxxxxxxxxxxxxxxxxxxxxxxxxxxxxxxxxxxxxxxxxxxx
d)		168[3]						182		175
25.	xxxxxxxxxxxxxxxxxxxxxxxxxxxxxxxxxxxxxxxxxxxxxxxxxxxxxxxxxxxxxx
26.	xxxxxxxxxxxxxxxxxxxxxxxxxxxxxxxxxxxxxxxxxxxxxxxxxxxxxxxxxxxxxx
27.	165	163	158					121		138
28.	xxxxxxxxxxxxxxxxxxxxxxxxxxxxxxxxxxxxxxxxxxxxxxxxxxxxxxxxxxxxxx
29.	xxxxxxxxxxxxxxxxxxxxxxxxxxxxxxxxxxxxxxxxxxxxxxxxxxxxxxxxxxxxxx
30.	282	214	200	175	175	175	165		152	179
		161[2]
31.	xxxxxxxxxxxxxxxxxxxxxxxxxxxxxxxxxxxxxxxxxxxxxxxxxxxxxxxxxxxxxx
32.	xxxxxxxxxxxxxxxxxxxxxxxxxxxxxxxxxxxxxxxxxxxxxxxxxxxxxxxxxxxxxx
33.	xxxxxxxxxxxxxxxxxxxxxxxxxxxxxxxxxxxxxxxxxxxxxxxxxxxxxxxxxxxxxx
34.	xxxxxxxxxxxxxxxxxxxxxxxxxxxxxxxxxxxxxxxxxxxxxxxxxxxxxxxxxxxxxx
35.	xxxxxxxxxxxxxxxxxxxxxxxxxxxxxxxxxxxxxxxxxxxxxxxxxxxxxxxxxxxxxx
36.	xxxxxxxxxxxxxxxxxxxxxxxxxxxxxxxxxxxxxxxxxxxxxxxxxxxxxxxxxxxxxx
37.	xxxxxxxxxxxxxxxxxxxxxxxxxxxxxxxxxxxxxxxxxxxxxxxxxxxxxxxxxxxxxx
38.	xxxxxxxxxxxxxxxxxxxxxxxxxxxxxxxxxxxxxxxxxxxxxxxxxxxxxxxxxxxxxx
39.	xxxxxxxxxxxxxxxxxxxxxxxxxxxxxxxxxxxxxxxxxxxxxxxxxxxxxxxxxxxxxx
Median	169	163	179	162	184	187	167	169	167	175
Mean
1967 $ Value	754	721	792	698	793	806	739	738	746	803

	1895	1896	1897	1898	1899	1900	1901	1902	1903	1904
1.	xxxxxxxxxxxxxxxxxxxxxxxxxxxxxxxxxxxxxxxxxxxxxxxxxxxxxxxxxxxxx
2.	193[3]		170[3]		173					
3.	xxxxxxxxxxxxxxxxxxxxxxxxxxxxxxxxxxxxxxxxxxxxxxxxxxxxxxxxxxxxx
4.				197						
5.	xxxxxxxxxxxxxxxxxxxxxxxxxxxxxxxxxxxxxxxxxxxxxxxxxxxxxxxxxxxxx
6.	xxxxxxxxxxxxxxxxxxxxxxxxxxxxxxxxxxxxxxxxxxxxxxxxxxxxxxxxxxxxx
7.	xxxxxxxxxxxxxxxxxxxxxxxxxxxxxxxxxxxxxxxxxxxxxxxxxxxxxxxxxxxxx
8.									270	
9.								136		
10.
11.		168	174			185				
12.
13.	xxxxxxxxxxxxxxxxxxxxxxxxxxxxxxxxxxxxxxxxxxxxxxxxxxxxxxxxxxxxx
14.	xxxxxxxxxxxxxxxxxxxxxxxxxxxxxxxxxxxxxxxxxxxxxxxxxxxxxxxxxxxxx
15.
16.
17.			193					238		
18.			183							
19.	xxxxxxxxxxxxxxxxxxxxxxxxxxxxxxxxxxxxxxxxxxxxxxxxxxxxxxxxxxxxx
20.	xxxxxxxxxxxxxxxxxxxxxxxxxxxxxxxxxxx
21.			167							
22.	xxxxxxxxxxxxxxxxxxxxxxxxxxxxxxxxxxxxxxxxxxxxxxxxxx
23.				194			185	267		
24.
a)	xxxxxx								152[1]	
b)		130								
c)
d)		144								
25.	xxxxxxxxxxxxxxxxxxxxxxxxxxxxxxxxxxxxxxxxxxxxxxxxxxxxxxxxxxxxx
26.	xxxxxxxxxxxxxxxxxxxxxxxxxxxxxxxxxxxxxxxxxxxxxxxxxxxxxxxxxxxxx
27.
28.	xxxxxxxxxxxxxxxxxxxxxxxxxxxxxxxxxxxxxxxxxxxxxxxxxxxxxxxxxxxxx
29.	xxxxxxxxxxxxxxxxxxxxxxxxxxxxxxxxxxxxxxxxxxxxxxxxxxxxxxxxxxxxx
30.			190	217				175	200	
31.	xxxxxxxxxxxxxxxxxxxxxxxxxxxxxxxxxxxxxxxxxxxxxxxxxxxxxxxxxxxxx
32.	xxxxxxxxxxxxxxxxxxxxxxxxxxxxxxxxxxxxxxxxxxxxxxxxxxxxxxxxxxxxx
33.	xxxxxxxxxxxxxxxxxxxxxxxxxxxxxxxxxxxxxxxxx
34.	xxxxxxxxxxxxxxxxxxxxxxxxxxxxxxxxxxxxxxxxxxxxxxxxxxxxxxxxxxxxx
35.	xxxxxxxxxxxxxxxxxxxxxxxxxxxxxxxxxxxxxxxxxxxxxxxxxxxxxxxxxxxxx
36.	xxxxxxxxxxxxxxxxxxxxxxxxxxxxxxxxxxxxxxxxxxxxxxxxxxxxxxxxxxxxx
37.	xxxxxxxxxxxxxxxxxxxxxxxxxxxxxxxxxxxxxxxxxxxxxxxxxxxxxxxxxxxxx
38.	xxxxxxxxxxxx
39.	xxxxxxxxxxxxxxxxxxxxxxxxxxxxxxxxxxxxxxxxxxxxxxxxxxxxxxxxxxxxx

Median
| | 193 | 168 | 172 | 197 | 173 | 185 | 185 | 206 | 200 |

Mean

1967 $ Value
| | 885 | 760 | 768 | 879 | 755 | 777 | 758 | 824 | 763 |

	1905	1906	1907	1908	1909	1910	1911	1912	1913	1914

1. xxxxxxxxxxxxxxxxxxxxxxxxxxxxxxxxxxxxxxxxxxxxxxxxxxxxxxxxxxxxxx
2.
3. xxxxxxxxxxxxxxxxxxxxxxxxxx
4.
5. xxxxxxxxxxxxxxxxxxxxxxxxxxxxxxxxxxxxxxxxxxxxxxxxxxxxxxxxxxxxxx
6. xxxxxxxxxxxxxxxxxxxxxxxxxxxxxxxxxxxxxxxxxxxxxxxxxxxxxxxxxxxxxx
7. xxxxxxxxxxxxxxxxxxxxxxxxxxxxxxxxxxxxxxxxxxxxxxxxxxxxxxxxxxxxxx
8.
9.
10.
11.
12.
13. xxxxxxxxxxxxxxxxxxxxxxxxxxxxxxxxxxxxxxxxxxxxxxxxxxxxxxxxxxxx
14. xxxxxxxxxxxxxx
15.
16.
17.
18.
19. xxxxxxxxxxxxxxxxxxxxxxxxxxxxxxxxxxxxxxxxxxxxxxxxxxxxxxxxxxxxxx
20.
21.
22.   195
23.
24.
  a)
  b)
  c)
  d)
25. xxxxxxxxxxxxxxxxxxxxxxxxxxxxxxxxxxxxxxxxxxxxxxxx
26.
27.
28. xxxxxxxxxxxxxxxxxxxxxxxxxxxx
29. xxxxxxxxxxxxxx
30.
31. xxxxxxxxxxxxxx
32. xxxxxxxxxxxxxxxxxxxxxxxxxxxxxxxxxxxxxxxxxxxxxxxxxxxxxxxxxxxxxx
33.
34. xxxxxxxxxxxxxxxxxxxxxxxxxxxxxxxxxxxxxxxxxxxxxxxxxxxxxxxxxxxxxx
35. xxxxxxxxxxxxxxxxxxxxxxxxxxxxxxxxxxxxxxxxxxxxxxxxxxxxxxxxxxxxxx
36. xxxxxxxxxxxxxxxxxxxxxxxxxxxxxxxxxxxxxxxxx
37. xxxxxxxxxxxxxxxxxxxxxxxxxxxxxxxxxxxxxxxxxxxxxxxxxxxxxxxx
38.
39. xxxxxxxxxxxxxxxxxxxxxxxxxxxxxxxxxxxxxxxxxxxxxxx

Median
                                                195

Mean

1967 $ Value
                                                720

	1915	1916	1917	1918	1919	1920	1921	1922	1923	1924
1.	xxxxxxxxxxxxxxxxxxxxxxxxxxx									
2.								297		
3.	361							385		
4.	251							503		
5.	xxxxxxxxxxxxxxxxxxxxxxxxxxxxxxxxxxxxxxxxx									
6.	xxxxxxxxxxxxxxxxxxxxxxxxxxxxxxxxxxxxxxxxxxxxxxxxxxxxxxxxxxxxxxxxxxxxxxxxxxxxx									
7.	xxxxxxxxxxxxxxxxxxxxxxxxxxxxxxxxxxxxx							389		
8.	159							276		
9.								206		
10.	174							558		
11.	147							194		
12.	229							253		
13.	xxxxxxxxxxxxxxxxxxx							390		
14.	267							379		
15.	177									
16.	192							333		
17.								525		
18.								240		
19.	xxxxxxxxxxxxxxxxxxxxxxxxxxxxxxxxxxxx							714		
20.								533		
21.	148							142		
22.								320		
23.	216							343		
24.	174							287		
a)										
b)										
c)					150					
d)										
25.	308							359		
26.	216							312		
27.	142							188		
28.	247									
29.	217							166		
30.	216							270		
31.	348							359		
32.	xxxxxxxxxxxxxxxxxxxx							386		
33.	216							383		
34.	xxxxxxxxxxxxx							203		
35.								304		
36.								204		
37.	184							451		
38.								263		
39.								184		

Median
    216
Mean
    183   306
1967 $ Value
    706   606

	1925	1926	1927	1928	1929	1930	1931
1.		223	241	291			
2.		257	262	262			
3.		366	375	395			
4.		610	611	559			
5.		364	354	335			
6.		664	846	696			
7.		454	416	326			
8.		229	357	260			
9.		223	214	233			
10.		257	319	301			
11.		282	293	287			
12.		225	240	215			
13.		283	358	342			
14.			332	336			
15.							
16.		359	371	348			
17.		283	306	287			
18.		250	256	254			
19.		321	285				
20.		580					
21.		193	187	189			
22.		349	349	345			
23.		389	402	434			
24.		332	332	334			
a)		356					
b)		303					
c)		305					
d)		374					
25.			288	262			
26.		330	318	331			
27.		218	217	225			
28.		206	176	190			
29.		208	207	246			
30.		249	296	297			
31.		402	323	309			
32.		312	301	280			
33.		468	523	433			
34.		257	242	204			
35.		279	261	260			
36.		177	184	190			
37.		200	206	430			
38.		311	307	287			
39.		317	253	396			
Median							
Mean		289	304	301	281	265	288
1967 $ Value		542	581	582	544	526	627

TABLE II

Mean Per Capita Maintenance Expenditures in United States Public Institutions for the Mentally Retarded 1926-1966

	Per Capita Maint. Expend. National Average	Per Capita Maint. Expend. in terms of 1967 $ Value
1926	289	542
1927	304	581
1928	301	582
1929	281	544
1930	265	526
1931	288	627
1932	263	638
1933	238	610
1934	237	587
1935	252	609
1936	259	620
1937	279	644
1938	296	696
1939	299	714
1940	291	690
1941	288	649
1942	315	640
1943	347	665
1944	365	689
1945	386	712
1946	434	739
1947	528	787
1948	631	873
1949	698	976
1950	746	1032
1951	807	1035
1952	920	1154
1953	980	1219
1954	1039	1287
1955	1093	1359
1956	1166	1428
1957	1280	1516
1958	1409	1623
1959	1503	1716
1960	1660	1868
1961	1742	1939
1962	1859	2045
1963	1995	2167
1964	2219	2381
1965	2380	2513
1966	2611	2676

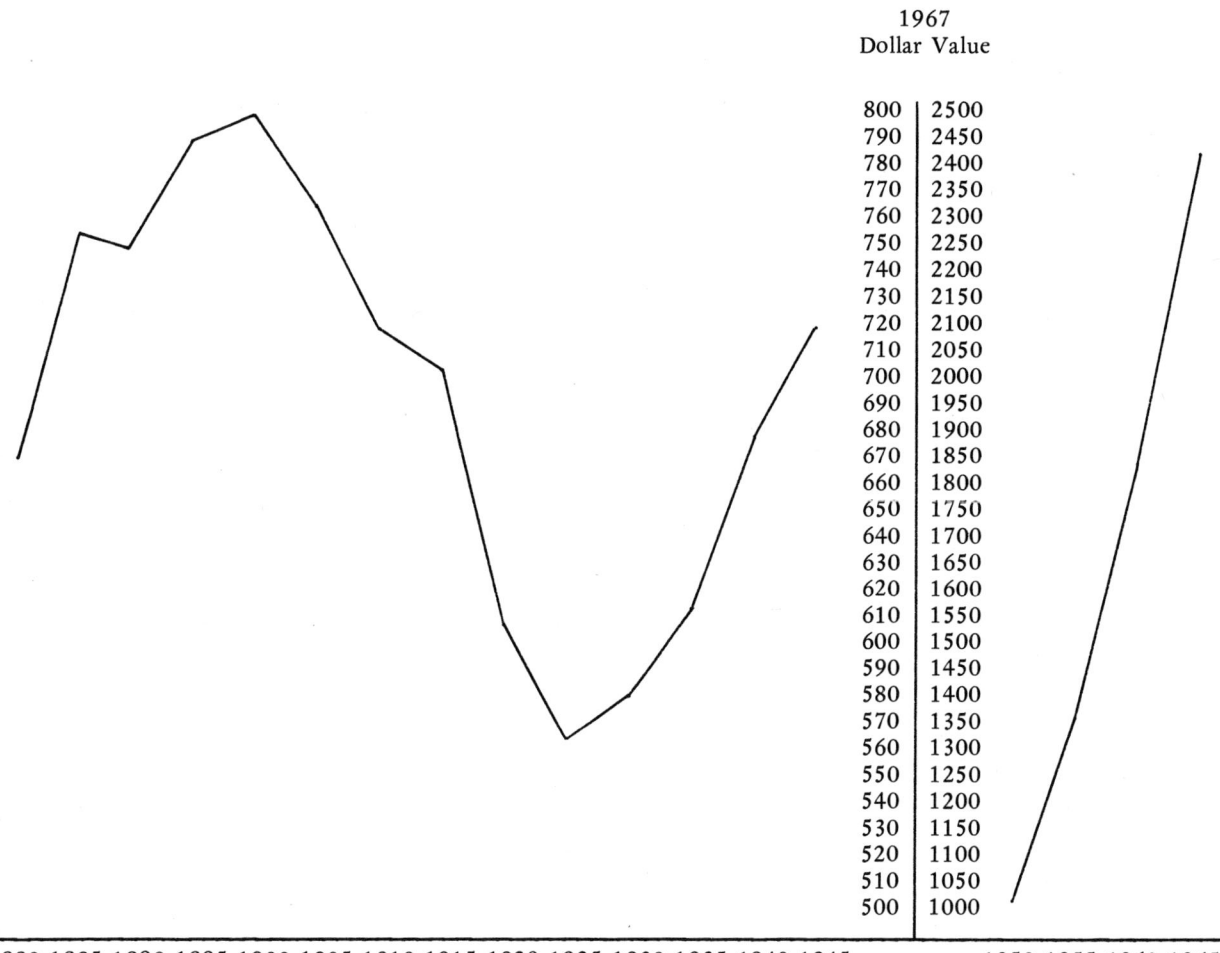

FIGURE 2: Five-Year Average of Annual Per Capita Maintenance Costs of Publicly Supported U.S. Institutions for the Mentally Retarded, 1878-1967, in Terms of 1967 Dollar Value.

Appendix 2

Origins of certain institutional features.

When we look at our institutions today, we are sometimes baffled by certain features we perceive. In the review of historical sources, I came across material that explains many of these features. This Appendix will present some of this material which underlines several of the points made earlier in the body of the review.

The incredible catch-all nature of the institution developed in the pity period; as usual, it was rationalized to be of benefit to the resident: "The probability is that, because of the peculiar adaptation of feeble-minded persons to a community organization, State institutions may be created to embrace the care of all whose dependence needs it, and inclusive, too, of all the multiform grades; for it seems despotic to omit those who are epileptic, paralytic, or choleric, permitting a physical impediment to bar the individual from beneficial influences to which he is as responsive as any. This all-comprehending care has been contemplated in Pennsylvania under the suggestion of an asylum village to be developed from the (base) already existing at Elwyn" (Kerlin, 1884, p. 259).

Monotony of design was advocated by Sprattling (1903, p. 265): "... at the Craig Colony, in New York, under the advice of eminent architects, thirty-seven cottages, comprising the main groups in the male and female divisions, are similar in exterior design and internal arrangement ..." Sprattling also advocated elimination of risks in the environment, such elimination being characteristic of the sub-human and medical models: "Some special constructional features should be incorporated, the more prominent of these being stairways broken by landings, to prevent patients from falling the entire length. All woodwork should have the sharp corners and angles broadly rounded to lessen the danger of cuts from falls during attacks; and all steam and hotwater pipes and radiators should be effectively covered or guarded, to prevent burning during coma following a seizure" (Sprattling, 1903, p. 266).

Sometimes we wonder where the term and concept of "back ward" comes from. During the pity period, when institutions experienced their first major enlargments, Pennsylvania erected two clusters of buildings for 500 residents. These clusters were a third of a mile apart, and the furthermost was reached by means of a narrow gage railway. That remote cluster of buildings housed the more severely retarded residents. The same concept of moving the most deviant person the farthest away is apparent in the following excerpt: "Before a blow is struck in the building of a colony, a definite plan of development should be laid out by marking a complete topographical map of the colony estate, always remembering the value of *approximating the main features;* and we may illustrate the methods of doing this by drawing a circle of sufficient diameter and putting in it the office building, the hospital, the laboratory, the chapel, the laundry, schools, storehouses, industries, library, and some employees' homes. Then draw another circle and let that embrace homes for the better class of patients; then a third for patients of the great middle class, and beyond that still the homes of cases relegated to infirmary care" (Sprattling, 1903, pp. 269-270).

One of the most extensive treatises on institutional design was offered by Wallace (1924). His proposals incorporate many principles of the subhuman and medical models: "The plan I have the honor of presenting to the Association today through the courtesy of the Board of Architects embodies the plan of the Wrentham State School as prepared 15 years ago, brought up to our present conception of what a plan for a School for the Feeble-Minded should be today by the addition of certain buildings which experience has convinced the writer are necessary to properly round out the institution.

"In presenting this plan the writer makes no claim of originality. In the working out of it, he is deeply indebted to builders of institutions in widely separated sections of the country. Especially is he indebted to his old Chief, the Dean of this Association. Many of you who have visited Waverley will recognize the adaptation of the Waverley dormitory buildings in this plan.

" . . . the Board of Architects, with whom it has been the writer's pleasure to work in developing this plan, has specialized in institutional construction for over 30 years" (pp. 266-268).

"The type of construction should be first class fire proof throughout, . . . using stone for foundation, outside steps, window sills, and water tables, using brick, hollow wall construction for the super structure and reinforced concrete for all walls and verandas, and using either brick or concrete for all cross walls with door frames made fast by strong anchors securely built into the masonry. Terra Cotta or hollow tile construction should not be used for cross walls, it is too brittle to stand the slamming of doors. If it is used, the door frames will work loose with a consequent breaking of the plaster around the doors" (p. 260).

"The lower five feet of all plastered walls should be Portland cement plaster which will stand rough usage without breaking" (p. 264).

"All of the electric light switches should be placed outside of the wards and dayrooms in the halls, 6 feet from the floor thus making it inconvenient for the children to meddle with them" (p. 264).

"The hot water supply pipes should be of adequate size to enable bathing to be carried on simultaneously throughout the whole institution on every floor of every building. In every building in which the children live there should be placed on the hot water supply at a point beyond where the hot water is taken off for dish washing, a control or anti-scalding valve, maintaining the temperature of the water at not over 100 degrees Farenheit, thus reducing to the minimum the danger of scalding" (pp. 263-264).

"All underground steam pipes, hot water pipes, refrigeration pipes, electric light wires and telephone wires, should be carried in a tunnel large enough for one to walk through and wide enough in which to properly use tools when making necessary repairs. Any other form of caring for this underground construction will, eventually, prove most costly and unsatisfactory.

"In an institution that will cost approximately $2,000,000—a tunnel to accommodate this construction will cost approximately $65,000. This cannot be considered exorbitant if looked upon as insurance against accident and deterioration, to those vital arteries through which course the heat, light and power of the institution" (p. 262).

"Much study should be given to the standardization, as far as possible, of all buildings, furnishings and equipment. It is desirable to have the buildings standardized for the largest part of the population. The window glass should be of uniform size throughout the institution. All hardware, plumbing, plumbing fixtures, faucets and all steam fixtures such as traps, and valves, should be standardized. All furnishings such as electric light fixtures, window shades, chairs, tables, bureaus, beds and bedding should also be standardized" (p. 259).

"The dormitory building can be the same for the two sexes and of standard size and construction" (p. 264).

"A standard dormitory to accommodate 105 pupils seems to combine economy of construction with efficiency in management" (p. 265).

"It is with some trepidation that I approach the problem of floors for in the history of institutional construction I presume no one subject has received more thorough discussion, yet the problem is not wholly solved . . . In hallways, bathrooms, diningrooms and dayrooms for adult working boys, I believe terrazzo has no equal. For adults' wards and dayrooms where very little water is required heavy battleship linoleum securely cemented to concrete underfloor may be used to advantage. For wards and dayrooms for low grade, untidy patients, where floors require frequent wiping up of spots, the rubber flooring is unsurpassed.

"In every institution, however, there is a large number of destructive patients who will move anything that is movable and destroy anything that is not indestructible.

"Linoleum and rubber flooring in a building for these patients are not satisfactory inasmuch as the patients will quickly have the linoleum and rubber separated from the under surface and broken and destroyed. In building for this class the flooring should be made of terrazzo everywhere except in the sleeping wards. Here, first class maple flooring seems to serve the purpose best. Kitchen floors should be of first quality slate, although a terrazzo floor here is satisfactory. A well troweled granolithic makes a satisfactory laundry floor. Rubber flooring throughout would make the most serviceable, quiet, and suitable covering for the school building. If this is too expensive, a satisfactory treatment is to have all halls and toilet rooms laid in terrazzo and school rooms with maple flooring. The best floor covering for the Assembly Hall is rubber. Again, if this is too expensive, heavy, battleship linoleum, securely cemented on a concrete under floor is quite satisfactory.

"In the hospital on account of its noiselessness, the ease with which it can be cared for, and because of its non-absorbent qualities, the free use of rubber flooring is justified, even though it may be expensive . . . most of the stairs throughout the institution should be steel with ¼" rubber inset treads securely cemented in place.

"In the buildings for destructive patients, the stairs should be built of either terrazzo or concrete" (pp. 260-262).

"There are certain institution buildings where one floor construction is clearly indicated. These are infirmary and nursery buildings where there should be no steps, the floor being located at but a slight elevation above the outside grade, and the building entered by means of slightly graded ramps. The laundry buildings should be on one floor, consisting of one large room. This makes the supervision by one person easily possible" (pp. 265-266).

In contrast to the specification of residents' living units stand the guidelines for employees' living quarters: "In planning and developing an institution it is of vital importance that the living quarters of the employees should have due consideration. No matter how Utopian a State Government, Board of Trustees, Superintendent or Medical Staff may be in their expressed desire of what shall be done for the benefit of the children in the institution, what is actually accomplished is what the employees do for the children. The higher the scale of intelligence and the higher the living ideals of the employees of an institution the higher degree of service will they render in caring for the children. Hence, how important it is to make housing and living conditions such as will attract to the service and retain in the service, the highest type of employee. Small, attractive, homes to accommodate about 20 employees each should be conveniently located throughout the grounds. These should consist of single room arrangements with good bath and toilet conveniences provided and a common reception room. These small homes make possible the gathering together of groups of congenial people. There should also be provided a number of small cottages for married employees. There should be a recreational center, — in fact, an up to date, well furnished club, consisting of a large common lounge, reading room, smoking room, pool room, bowling alleys, and a store. The officers' quarters should be a little village of small houses that could be occupied by the families of married officers or five to seven single officers. In this center should be a building designed for kitchen, dining room and recreational purposes" (p. 266).

References

Account of the ceremonies at the laying of the cornerstone of the New York asylum for idiots, at Syracuse, September 8, 1854. Albany: J. Munsell, 1854.

American Medical Association. *Mental retardation: a handbook for the primary physician.* Chicago: American Medical Association, 1965.

Anderson, M. L. Instruction of the feebleminded. *Conf. Social Work,* 1918, 536-543.

Anonymous. A mother writes her impressions on Sonoma. *The Challenger,* 1968, *2* (3), 5.

Bancroft, M. Classification of the mentally deficient. *Proc. Nat. Conf. Charities & Correction,* 1901, 191-200.

Barr, M. W. President's annual address. *J. Psycho-Asthenics,* 1897, *2,* 1-13.

Barr M. W. The how, the why, and the wherefore of the training of feebleminded children. *J. Psycho-Asthenics,* 1899, *4,* 204-212.

Barr, M. W. The imbecile and epileptic *versus* the tax-payer and the community. *Proc. Nat. Conf. Charities & Correction,* 1902, 161-165. (a)

Barr, M. W. The imperative call of our present to our future. *J. Psycho-Asthenics,* 1902, *7,* 5-14. (b)

Barr, M. W. *Mental defectives, their history, treatment, and training.* Philadelphia: P. Blakiston's Son & Co., 1904.

Barr, M. W. Results of asexualization. *J. Psycho-Asthenics,* 1905, *9,* 129.

Barr, M. W. The prevention of mental defect, the duty of the hour. *Proc. Nat. Conf. Charities & Correction,* 1915, 361-367.

Barrows, S. J. Discussion on provision for the feeble-minded. *Proc. Nat. Conf. Charities & Correction,* 1888, 396-404.

Bartlett, F. L. Institutional peonage, our exploitation of mental patients. *Atlantic Monthly,* 1964, *214* (1), 116-119.

Bartlett, F. L. Present-day requirements for state hospitals joining the community. *New Eng. J. Med.,* 1967, *276,* 90-94.

Bayes, K. *The therapeutic effect of environment on emotionally disturbed and mentally subnormal children: A Kaufmann international design award 1964-66.* Old Woking (Surrey, England): The Gresham Press, 1967.

Beedy, Helen C. Discussion on the care of the feeble-minded. *Proc. Nat. Conf. Charities & Correction,* 1895, 467-468.

Bernstein, C. Minutes. *J. Psycho-Asthenics,* 1913, *18,* 59.

Bernstein, C. Rehabilitation of the mentally defective. *J. Psycho-Asthenics,* 1918, *23,* 92-94. (a)

Bernstein, C. Self-sustaining feeble-minded. *J. Psycho-Asthenics,* 1918, *22,* 150-161. (b)

Bernstein, C. Colony and extra-institutional care for the feeble-minded. *Conf. Social Work,* 1920, 359-367.

Bicknell, E. P. Custodial care of the adult feeble-minded. *J. Psycho-Asthenics,* 1896, *1,* 51-63.

Bliss, G. S. The cottage plan in the care of the feeble-minded. *J. Psycho-Asthenics,* 1913, *18,* 139-141.

Bonsall, A. Discussion on the care of imbeciles. *Proc. Nat. Conf. Charities & Correction,* 1891, 331-332.

Brewer, W. H. Discussion on the care of the feeble-minded. *Proc. Nat. Conf. Charities & Correction,* 1895, 467.

Brown, Mrs. G. Public aid for the feeble-minded. *Proc. Nat. Conf. Charities & Correction,* 1889, 86-88.

Bullard, W. N. State care of high-grade imbecile girls. *Proc. Nat. Conf. Charities & Correction,* 1910, 299-303. (a)

Bullard, W. N. The high grade mental defectives. *J. Psycho-Asthenics,* 1910, *14,* 14-15. (b)

Butler, A. W. The burden of feeble-mindedness. *Proc. Nat. Conf. Charities & Correction,* 1907, 1-10.

Butler, A. W. The feeble-minded: the need for research. *Proc. Nat. Conf. Charities & Corrections,* 1915, 356-361.

Butler, F. C. Tuberculosis in Sonoma State Home. *California & West. Med.,* 1944, *61,* 98-99.

Byers, A. G. Discussion on care of feeble-minded. *Proc. Nat. Conf. Charities & Correction,* 1890, 441.

Byers, J. P. A state plan for the care of the feeble-minded. *Proc. Nat. Conf. Charities & Correction,* 1916, 223-229.

Carson, J. C. Prevention of feeble-mindedness from a moral and legal standpoint. *Proc. Nat. Conf. Charities & Correction,* 1898, 294-303.

Carson, J. C. Review of legislation for defectives in the United States for the year, 1905. *J. Psycho-Asthenics,* 1906, *11,* 36-38.

Cave, F. C. Report of sterilization in the Kansas State Home for the feeble-minded. *J. Psycho-Asthenics,* 1911, *15,* 123-125.

Clark, A. W. Reports from States, *Proc. Nat. Conf. Charities & Correction,* 1901, 74-78.

Cleland, C. C., & Peck, R. F. Intra-institutional administrative problems: a paradigm for employee stimulation. *Ment. Retard.,* 1967, 5(3), 2-8.

Constitution and by-laws of the Massachusetts school for idiotic and feeble-minded youth. Boston: Cross & Freeman, Printers, 1851.

Cornell, W. S. Methods of preventing feeble-mindedness. *Proc. Nat. Conf. Charities & Correction,* 1915, 328-339.

Crookshank, F. G. *The mongol in our midst: a study of man and his three faces.* London: Kegan Paul, Trench, Trubner & Co., 1924.

Davies, S. P. *Social control of the feeble-minded: a study of social programs and attitudes in relation to the problem of mental deficiency.* New York: National Committee for Mental Hygiene, 1923.

Davies, S. P. *Social control of the mentally deficient.* New York: Thomas Y. Crowell Co., 1930.

DeProspo, C. J. Habilitation of the retardate. In W. A. Fraenkel (Ed.), *Proceedings: First Brooklyn Medical Conference on Mental Retardation.* New York: Assoc. for Help of Retarded Children, 1966.

Deutsch, A. *The mentally ill in America: a history of their care and treatment from colonial times.* (2nd ed.). New York: Columbia University Press, 1949.

Dunlap, M. J. Progress in the care of the feeble-minded and epileptics. *Proc. Nat. Conf. Charities & Correction,* 1899, 255-259.

Dunphy, M. C. Modern ideals of education applied to the training of mental defectives. *Proc. Nat. Conf. Charities & Correction,* 1908, 325-333.

Emerich, E. J. Minutes. *J. Psycho-Asthenics,* 1917, *21,* 112. (a)

Emerich, E. J. Progress in the care of the feeble-minded in Ohio. *J. Psycho-Asthenics,* 1917, *22,* 73-79. (b)

Estabrook, A. H. The pauper idiot pension in Kentucky. *J. Psycho-Asthenics,* 1928, *33,* 59-61.

Fernald, W. E. The history of the treatment of the feeble-minded. *Proc. Nat. Conf. Charities & Correction,* 1893, 203-221.

Fernald, W. E. The Massachusetts farm colony for the feeble-minded. *Proc. Nat. Conf. Charities & Correction,* 1902, 487-490.

Fernald, W. E. Care of the feeble-minded. *Proc. Nat. Conf. Charities & Correction,* 1904, 380-390.

Fernald, W. E. Discussions. *J. Psycho-Asthenics,* 1908, *13,* 116.

Fernald, W. E. The burden of feeble-mindedness. *J. Psycho-Asthenics,* 1912, *17,* 87-111.

Fernald, W. E. What is practical in the way of prevention of mental defect? *Proc. Nat. Conf. Charities & Correction,* 1915, 289-297.

Fernald, W. E. A state program for the care of the mentally defective. *Ment. Hyg.,* 1919, *3,* 566-574. (a)

Fernald, W. E. State programs for the care of the mentally defective. *J. Psycho-Asthenics,* 1919, *24,* 114-125. (b)

Fernald, W. E. An out-patient clinic in connection with a state institution for the feeble-minded. *J. Psycho-Asthenics,* 1920, *25,* 81-89.

Fernald, W. E. Thirty years progress in the care of the feeble-minded. *J. Psycho-Asthenics,* 1924, *29,* 206-219.

Fish, W. B. The colony plan. *Proc. Nat. Conf. Charities & Correction,* 1892, 161-165. (a)

Fish, W. B. Report of the committee on rules of procedure: discussion. *Proc. Nat. Conf. Charities & Correction,* 1892, 337-350. (b)

Fitts, A. M. How to fill the gap between the special classes and institutions. *J. Psycho-Asthenics,* 1915, *20,* 78-87.

Follett, M.D. Discussion on the care of the feeble-minded. *Proc. Nat. Conf. Charities & Correction,* 1895, 462.

Fox. Discussion. *Proc. Nat. Conf. Charities & Correction,* 1900, 430-431.

Goddard, H. H. Discussion. *Proc. Nat. Conf. Charities & Correction,* 1912, 283-284. (a)

Goddard, H. H. *The Kallikak Family.* New York: Macmillan, 1912. (b)

Goddard, H. H. The possibilities of research as applied to the prevention of feeble-mindedness. *Proc. Nat. Conf. Charities & Correction,* 1915, 307-312.

Greene, H. H. M. The obligation of civilized society to idiotic and feeble-minded children. *Proc. Nat. Conf. Charities & Correction,* 1884, 264-271.

Greene, R. A. An ideal institution organization for 1000 to 15,000 beds. *J. Psycho-Asthenics,* 1927, *32,* 186-192.

Harley, H. L. Observations on the operation of the Illinois commitment law for the feeble-minded. *J. Psycho-Asthenics,* 1917, *22,* 94-107.

Hart. Discussion of Mr. Bicknell's paper. *Proc. Nat. Conf. Charities & Correction,* 1896, 487-489.

Hastings, G. A. Registration of the feeble-minded. *Conf. Social Work,* 1918, *527,* 536.

Howe, S. G. *Report made to the legislature of Massachusetts upon idiocy.* Boston, Mass.: Collidge & Wiley, 1848.

Howe, S. G. *Third and final report on the experimental school for teaching and training idiotic children; also, the first report of the trustees of the Massachusetts school for idiotic and feeble-minded youth.* Cambridge, Mass.: Metcalf and Company, 1852.

Howe, S. G. *In ceremonies on laying the corner-stone of the New York State institution for the blind, at Batavia, Genesee Co., New York.* Batavia, N.Y.: Henry Todd, 1866.

Jaslow, R. I., Kime, W. L., & Green, M. J. Criteria for admission to institutions for the mentally retarded. *Ment. Retard.,* 1966, *4,* (4), 2-5.

Johnson, A. Discussion on care of the feeble-minded. *Proc. Nat. Conf. Charities & Correction,* 1889, 318-319.

Johnson, A. Permanent custodial care: report of the committee on the care of the feeble-minded. *Proc. Nat. Conf. Charities & Correction,* 1896, 207-219.

Johnson, A. Concerning a form of degeneracy. *Amer. J. Sociol.,* 1898, *4,* 463-473.

Johnson, A. Discussion. *J. Psycho-Asthenics,* 1899, *4,* 228-229.

Johnson, A. The self-supporting imbecile. *J. Psycho-Asthenics,* 1900, *4.* 91-100.

Johnson, A. Discussion on care of feeble-minded and epileptic. *Proc. Nat. Conf. Charities & Correction,* 1901, 410-411.

Johnson, A. Discussion on the feeble-minded and epileptic. *Proc. Nat. Conf. Charities & Correction,* 1902, 492-495.

Johnson, A. Report of committee on colonies for segregation of defectives. *Proc. Nat. Conf. Charities & Correction,* 1903, 245-253.

Johnson, A. Minutes and discussion. *Proc. Nat. Conf. Charities & Correction,* 1905, 536-537.

Johnson, A. Custodial care. *Proc. Nat. Conf. Charities & Correction,* 1908, 333-336.

Johnstone, E. R. President's address. *J. Psycho-Asthenics,* 1904, *8,* 63-68.

Johnstone, E. R. Defectives. Report of the committee. *Proc. Nat. Conf. Charities & Correction,* 1906, 235-243.

Johnstone, E. R. Discussions: *J. Psycho-Asthenics,* 1908, *13,* 113-115. (a)

Johnstone, E. R. Practical provision for the mentally deficient. *Proc. Nat. Conf. Charities & Correction,* 1908, 316-325. (b)

Johnstone, E. R. Discussion. State care of the feeble-minded. *J. Psycho-Asthenics,* 1913, *18,* 38-45

Johnstone, E. R. Committee report: stimulating public interest in the feeble-minded. *Proc. Nat. Conf. Charities & Correction,* 1916, 205-215.

Kaplan, O. Life expectancy of low grade mental defectives. *Psychol. Bull.,* 1939, *36,* 513. (Abstract)

Kerlin, I. N. Provision for idiotic and feeble-minded children. *Proc. Nat. Conf. Charities & Correction,* 1884, 246-263.

Kerlin, I. N. Report of standing committee. *Proc. Nat. Conf. Charities & Correction,* 1885, 158-178. (a)

Kerlin, I. N. Status of the work. *Proc. Assoc. Med. Offs. Amer. Insts. Idiotic Feeble-Minded Persons.* 1885, *9,* 369-372. (b)

Kerlin, I. N. Report of the committee on provision for idiotic and feeble-minded persons. *Proc. Nat. Conf. Charities & Correction,* 1886, 288-297.

Kerlin, I. N. Status of the work. *Proc. Assoc. Med. Offs. Amer. Insts. Idiotic Feeble-Minded Persons.* 1888, *12,* 81-82. (a)

Kerlin, I. N. Report of the committee on the care and training of the feeble-minded. *Proc. Nat. Conf. Charities & Correction,* 1888, 99-101. (b)

Kerlin, I. N. Discussion on care of feeble-minded. *Proc. Nat. Conf. Charities & Correction,* 1890, 444-445.

Kirkbride, F. B. Types of buildings for state institutions for the feeble-minded. *Proc. Nat. Conf. Charities & Correction,* 1916, 250-257.

Kirkland, M. H. Institutions for the retarded: their place in the continuum of services. *Ment. Retard.,* 1967, *5* (2), 5-8.

Knight, G. H. Colony care for adult idiots. *Proc. Nat. Conf. Charities & Correction,* 1891, 107-108.

Knight, G. H. Report of the committee on rules of procedure: Discussion. *Proc. Nat. Conf. Charities & Correction,* 1892, 348-349.

Knight, G. H. The feeble-minded. *Proc. Nat. Conf. Charities & Correction,* 1895, 150-159.

Knight, G. H. Prevention from a legal and moral standpoint. *Proc. Nat. Conf. Charities & Correction,* 1898, 304-308.

Knight, H. M. Status of the work. *Proc. Assoc. Med. Offs. Amer. Insts. Idiotic Feeble-Minded Persons,* 1879, *4,* 96.

Levinson, E. J. Professionals and parents, a study in changing attitudes. *Amer. J. Ment. Defic.,* 1960, *64,* 765-769.

Long. Discussion on care of feeble-minded. *Proc. Nat. Conf. Charities & Correction,* 1899, 407-408.

Mastin, J. T. The new colony plan for the feeble-minded. *Proc. Nat. Conf. Charities & Correction,* 1916, 239-250. (a)

Mastin, J. T. The new colony plan for the feeble-minded. *J. Psycho-Asthenics,* 1916, *21,* 25-35. (b)

McCready, E. B. The treatment of mental defectives through physical and medical measures. *J. Psycho-Asthenics,* 1918, *23.* 43-51.

Mertz, E. W. Mortality among the mentally deficient during a 20-50 year period. *Train. Sch. Bull.,* 1934, *30,* 185-197.

Murdoch, J. M. President's address. *J. Psycho-Asthenics,* 1903, *7,* 67-72.

Murdoch, J. M. Aims and possibilities of the new institution for feeble-minded and epileptics. *Proc. Nat. Conf. Charities & Correction,* 1906, 269-273.

Murdoch, J. M. Quarantine mental defectives. *Proc. Nat. Conf. Charities & Correction,* 1909, 64-67. (a)

Murdoch, J. M. Reports from States. *J. Psycho-Asthenics,* 1909, *14,* 139-140. (b)

Murdoch, J. M. Fundamental principles involved in the organization and construction of an institution for the feeble-minded. *J. Psycho-Asthenics,* 1930, *35,* 239-251.

Murdock, C. A. Discussion on the care of the feeble-minded. *Proc. Nat. Conf. Charities & Correction,* 1889, 312-317.

Murdock, J. M. Minutes. *J. Psycho-Asthenics,* 1917, *22,* 41-42.

Murdock, J. M. State care for the feeble-minded. *J. Psycho-Asthenics,* 1913, *18,* 34-38.

Nicholson, T. Discussion on the feeble-minded and epileptic. *Proc. Nat. Conf. Charities & Correction,* 1902, 495.

Nosworthy, N. Suggestions concerning the psychology of mentally deficient children. *J. Psycho-Asthenics,* 1907, *12,* 3-17.

Osborne, A. E. The founding of a great institution and some of its problems. *Proc. Assoc. Med. Offs. Amer. Insts. Idiotic Feeble-Minded Persons,* 1891, *15,* 173-185.

Penrose, L. S. *The biology of mental defect.* London: Sidgwick and Jackson Ltd., 1963.

Perry, M. E. Minority report. *Proc. Nat. Conf. Charities & Correction,* 1903, 253-254.

Pierson, S. S. Discussion on the care of imbeciles. *Proc. Nat. Conf.*

Charities & Correction, 1891, 331-337.

Polglase, W. A. Discussion. *Proc. Nat. Conf. Charities & Correction*, 1900, 425-426.

Polglase, W. A. The evolution of the care of the feeble-minded and epileptic in the past century. *Proc. Nat. Conf. Charities & Correction*, 1901, 186-190.

Powell, F. M. The care and training of feeble-minded children. *Proc. Nat. Conf. Charities & Correction*, 1887, 250-260.

Powell, F. M. Care of the feeble-minded. *Proc. Nat. Conf. Charities & Correction*, 1897, 289-302.

Reports from states. *Proc. Nat. Conf. Charities & Correction*, 1890, 329.

Reports from states. *Proc. Nat. Conf. Charities & Correction*, 1898, 53.

Reports from states. *Proc. Nat. Conf. Charities & Correction*, 1912, 525.

Richards, B. W. Pulmonary tuberculosis mortality in a mental deficiency hospital. *Amer. J. Ment. Defic.*, 1954, *59*, 245-253.

Risley, S. D. Is asexualization ever justifiable in the case of imbecile children? *J. Psycho-Asthenics*, 1905, *9*, 92-98.

Robinson, G. S. Reports from the states: *Illinois. Proc. 8th Annual Conf. Charities & Correction*, 1881, 51-55.

Rogers, A. C. Functions of a school for feeble-minded. *Proc. Nat. Conf. Charities & Correction*, 1888, 101-106.

Rogers, A. C. Does the education of the feeble-minded pay? *J. Psycho-Asthenics*, 1898, *2*, 152-154.

Schlapp, M. G. Available field for research and prevention in mental defect. *Proc. Nat. Conf. Charities & Correction*, 1915, 320-328.

Seguin, E. *New facts and remarks concerning idiocy.* New York: Wm. Wood & Co., 1870.

Seguin, E. Recent progress in the training of idiots. *Proc. Assoc. Med. Offs. Amer. Insts. Idiotic Feeble-Minded Persons*, 1878, *3*, 60-65.

Sharman, G. Do we "dehabilitate" the retarded? in J. D. Van Peit (Ed.), *Proc. Fifth Annual Interstate Conf. Ment. Defic.* Melbourne, Australia: Australian Group for the Scientific Study of Mental Deficiency, 1966.

Siegler, M., & Osmond, H. Models of madness. *Brit. J. Psychiat.*, 1966, *112*, 1193-1203.

Sloan, W. Four score and seven. *Amer. J. Ment. Defic.*, 1963, *68*, 6-14.

Smith, W. H. C. Discussion. *J. Psycho-Asthenics*, 1913, *18*, 39-40.

Southard, E. E. The feeble-minded as subjects of research in efficiency. *Proc. Nat. Conf. Charities & Correction*, 1915, 315-319.

Speyer, N. Social integration of the mentally handicapped adult. In International League of Societies for the Mentally Handicapped. *International Congress on the education and social integration of the mentally handicapped.* Brussels: Author, 1963, pp. 155-165.

Spratling, W. P. The remedial, economic, and ethical value of labor. *Proc. Nat. Conf. Charities & Correction*, 1889, 309-319.

Spratling, W. P. Discussion of care of feeble-minded and epileptic. *Proc. Nat. Conf. Charities & Correction*, 1901, 409-410.

Sprattling, W. E. An ideal colony for epileptics. *Proc. Nat. Conf. Charities & Correction*, 1903, 259-271.

Status of the work. *Proc. Assoc. Med. Offs. Amer. Insts. Idiotic Feeble-Minded Persons*, 1886, *10*, 442-462.

Stebbins, H. Discussion on care of the feeble-minded. *Proc. Nat. Conf. Charities & Correction*, 1889, 324-326.

Stewart, J. Q. Discussion on the feeble-minded. *Proc. Nat. Conf. Charities & Correction*, 1894, 310-311.

Stone, H. Report of the committee on rules of procedures: Discussion. *Proc. Nat. Conf. Charities & Correction*, 1892, 337-350.

Streeter, L. C. The relation of mental defect to the neglected, dependent, and delinquent children of New Hampshire. *Proc. Nat. Conf. Charities & Correction*, 1915, 340-352.

Swan, W. W. Address of welcome. *J. Psycho-Asthenics*, 1908, *12*, 62-70.

Taft, J. Supervision of the feeble-minded in the community. *Conf. Social Work*, 1918, 543-550.

Taylor, J. M. Hints to the officers of institutions for the feeble-minded. *J. Psycho-Asthenics*, 1898, *3*, 76-81.

Theodos, P. A. Tuberculosis in the feeble-minded. *Amer. Rev. Tub.*, 1948, *58*, 237-249.

Tizard, J. *Community services for the mentally handicapped.* London: Oxford University Press, 1964.

Van Wagenen, B. Surgical sterilization as a eugenic measure. *J. Psycho-Asthenics*, 1914, *18*, 185-196.

Vail, D. J. *Dehumanization and the institutional career.* Springfield, Ill.: Charles C. Thomas, 1967.

Walk, J. W. Discussion on care of feeble-minded. *Proc. Nat. Conf. Charities & Correction*, 1890, 440-441.

Wallace, G. L. Plan and construction of an institution for feeble-minded. *J. Psycho-Asthenics*, 1928, *33*, 235-254.

Watkins, H. M. Administration in institutions of over two thousand, *J. Psycho-Asthenics*, 1928, *33*, 235-254.

Wells, K. State regulation of marriage. *Proc. Nat. Conf. Charities & Correction*, 1897, 302-308.

Wilbur, C. T. Institutions for the feeble-minded: the result of forty years of effort in establishing them in the United States. *Proc. Nat. Conf. Charities & Correction*, 1888, 106-113.

Wilbur, H. B. Status of the work. *Proc. Assoc. Med. Offs. Amer. Insts. Idiotic Feeble-Minded Persons*, 1879, *4*, 96.

Wilkins, L. T. *Social deviance: social policy, action, and research.* Englewood Cliffs, N.J.: Prentice-Hall, Inc., 1965.

Wilmarth, A. W. Institution construction and organization. *J. Psycho-Asthenics*, 1900, *5*, 58-64.

Wilmarth, A. W. Report of committee on feeble-minded and epileptic. *Proc. Nat. Conf. Charities & Correction*, 1902, 152-161.

Windle, C. Prognosis of mental subnormals. *Amer. J. Ment. Defic. Monogr. Suppl.*, 1962, *66*, No. 5.

Wines, F. H. Discussion on care of the feeble-minded. *Proc. Nat. Conf. Charities & Correction*, 1889, 319-324.

Winspear, C. W. The protection and training of feeble-minded women. *Proc. Nat. Conf. Charities & Correction*, 1895, 160-163.

Footnotes

1. This essay evolved from a series of lectures and an address given before the Wisconsin Association for Retarded Children, Janesville, Wisconsin, May 1967. The writing of the paper was supported by U.S.P.H.S. Grant HD00370 from the National Institute of Child Health and Human Development. I am indebted to my colleagues, Psychiatrist Frank Menolascino and Sociologist Richard A. Kurtz (now at Notre Dame University) for inspiration and critical reading of earlier drafts.

    In this essay, I will attempt to define the nature of various models which appear to underlie the design, location, and operation of residential facilities for the mentally retarded. I will then trace the historical evolution of various models that have been and are most prominent in the United States. In both tasks, I will rely heavily on original quotations, because I found that statements out of the past often have more direct impact than any attempts to rephrase or summarize them.

2. A similar attempt to relate psychiatric treatment approaches to schizophrenia to theoretical models can be found in Siegler and Osmond (1966). For a discussion of Osmond's collaborative efforts with architect Izumi to design buildings for residents rather than for other architects, see Bayes (1967).

3. There are several versions of this account, derived from the various editions of Luther's Tabletalks, e.g., *Luther's Works,* Vol. 54, Fortress Press, Philadelphia, 1967, p. 396, and Aurifaber, Jr., *Tischreden,* Vol. 5, Weimer Edition, p. 9. In all editions the account is item No. 5207.

4. Sloan (1963) brilliantly related the relevance of social movements to the history of mental retardation. However, his essay was not specifically concerned with institutions.

5. For a picture of the Massachusetts School for the Feeble-Minded in South Boston, see the *Proceedings of the Association of Medical Officers of American Institutions for Idiotic and Feeble-Minded Persons,* 1880, Vol. 5, p. 114.

6. An apparently widely held view was stated by Taylor (1898), who reasoned that if procreation was rendered impossible by surgery, there would be no further value in preserving the sexual instinct of the retarded. Since much harm was seen to result in the cultivation or even retention of this instinct, Taylor recommended that it would be just as well " . . . to remove the organs which the sufferers are unfit to exercise normally, and for which they are the worse in the unnatural cultivation or use" (p. 81). Thus, for males, castration was widely preferred over vasectomy (Cave, 1911; Van Wagenen, 1914). In one stroke it not only accomplished sterilization; it also eliminated "Sexual debaucheries" (Cave) and masturbation (Van Wagenen), and perhaps even improved "the singing voice" (Barr, 1905) and diminished epileptic seizures (Barr, 1904). Sometimes, castration was performed " . . . after exhausting every other means . . . " as a " . . . cure for masturbation," even without a perceived need for sterilization (Reports from States, 1895, p. 384). By 1914, sterilization was used not only for eugenic but also for penal reasons, sometimes in addition to a prison sentence. The courts upheld this measure as constituting neither cruel nor unusual punishment for certain crimes (Van Wagenen). In cases where vasectomy was performed, the retarded did "not require an anaesthetic since all that is required is to cut the *vas defrens*" (Risley, 1905, p. 97).

7. For a long time, tuberculosis and related diseases appear to have been the leading cause of death in institutions for the retarded (e.g., Barr, 1904; Butler, 1944; Kaplan, 1939; Martz, 1934; Richards, 1954; Theodos, 1948). It is interesting and revealing that the implications of this fact do not seem to have been adequately elaborated in the literature of the field.

8. It should be noted here that the growth of institutional places far exceeded the growth of the population. In 1904, there were 17.5 places per 100,000 population; in 1910 it had grown to 22.5; in 1923 it was 39.3; and by 1956 it had reached 66.1 (Davies, 1959). In 1966, it was 98.7. Furthermore, it should be noted that each bed during the indictment period could serve a much larger number of residents than today, because the turnover rate due to deaths was very high.